Make

Finding Hope: Faith for the Frustrated 3

Michael S. Rogers

WORDS MATTER
P U B L I S H I N G
OUR WORDS CHANGE THE WORLD

Words Matter Publishing
P.O. Box 1190
Decatur, IL 62525
www.wordsmatterpublishing.com

ISBN: 978-1-962467-91-9

Library of Congress Catalog Card Number: 2025939627

Dedication

For Randy Kirk, George Ross, and all the other
spiritual giants who have mentored me in
making disciples and leading a church.

Acknowledgements

This volume in the series would have been impossible without the love and support of my former church, Faith Church of Christ in Burlington, Indiana. Over the years, I was able to work with different elders who spoke into my ministry: Lance Alter, Sam Moffitt, Jon Newlin, Rick Helvie (God rest his soul), Jerry Bean, Scott Wagoner, Pat Amos, and Keith Lindley.

They healed us when we were hurting, supported us when we were learning, followed us when we were leading, and launched us when we were leaving. In the middle of that, I first taught some of this material and those who were serving as elders at the time attended every session.

For my "Lifers" (as they call themselves), here is the Living Grace series for you in print. I pray you share it with those you are discipline!

Table of Contents

PART 3: LIVE

Introduction

We were on a short holiday in Madison, a quaint little town on the Ohio River about as far south as we could go and still be in Indiana. We had been to a restaurant called Red, where a great chef and some soft jazz had filled our stomachs and our hearts, making us restless. Carrie suggested we go for a drive.

Night had fallen already, but we found ourselves cruising down a county highway along the river, talking about what God was doing in our lives. The church I pastored was firing on all cylinders. A great Sunday experience, small groups almost every night of the week, classes that discipled the Already Believers, and regular decisions by those Not Yet believers to give their hearts to Jesus. The leadership had voted to open a coffee shop in town as a third space ministry, and within the first few months, it was self-sustaining and becoming a major community gathering place.

We were doing everything right. But God…

The holiday was meant to be a break from the ministry, and truly, it was. Walking around the town and relaxing at dinner, we talked about life together: the kids, our marriage, our challenges, and dreams. But God was drawing us toward a calling. The conversation turned toward the restlessness we were feeling.

Nothing was going wrong at the church, but God was working on our hearts and showing us something we couldn't deny. The pandemic had convinced us that great Sunday morning gatherings were not enough. A complete change in the focus and dynamics of how we "church" was coming; changes that would be systemic, culture-altering, so different from what we were currently performing.

A change so big, we realized it wouldn't be fair to ask our great church to go through it. So much had already been asked of them. They had been so faithful as they not only gave permission to make the changes but championed them and protected me from those who complained. We had been looking for a house to buy, intending to minister there until I was ready to retire.

But God…

He used my frustration against me. Maybe that doesn't make sense after the successful ministry I just described—but hear me out. God hadn't changed, the church hadn't changed, my leadership hadn't changed, but I had. My definition of success wasn't the same.

Don't think of me as a visionary, though. Think of me as a frustrated pastor, using my frustration as motivation to be unhappy with a ministry any pastor would give his right arm to have. I wasn't in the right place mentally or spiritually, but God was using that to show me something. He took my weakness and, in His strength, birthed a new calling in my heart.

Then he surprised my wife by birthing that calling in her, too. She would be a greater part of the ministry than ever before, but she had to be convinced. A pastor's kid, a pastor's wife, and a pastor's mother she was already struggling with the roles she had been asked to play. But God...

After a fruitless search to find an established church that would fit our vision, we realized God was asking us to plant a new kind of church experience. As the car wound through the Indiana countryside and darkness fell, we talked about what God was showing us. Because we were still trying to understand what the ministry would look like, we turned to a discussion about what to name it. That seemed like a safe topic, but God...

At the time, we were thinking of planting in Florida near several bodies of water (people near the beaches need Jesus!). Carrie suggested *The Lake* would reference the area and give us some great imagery. I said something about *The Living Stone*, which now sounds like a dumb idea to me. She thought maybe *The Core* would demonstrate that we were the center of a movement, not just a church. I liked that.

But something had been birthing in me over the previous weeks. I had even checked online to see if many churches had the name and was surprised to find only one church in Muncie, Indiana, was using it. I liked the short simplicity of it, but I wasn't sure it would work. As we talked, we realized God was showing us a movement, not a church. The name would have to carry that weight. Could this?

Finally, I said, "I've been thinking about this name for a while, but I don't know if it's right. What do you think about *The Jar?*"

I couldn't see her face because no streetlights lined that old Indiana highway. Complete darkness covered us as we traveled between towns and came around a curve. Suddenly, the darkness was interrupted by a lone sign glaring in the late evening gloom. A church sign with one verse on it.

> *For I know the plans I have for you, declares the Lord, plans for good and not for evil, to give you a future and a hope.*
>
> — *Jeremiah 29:11*

We sat in stunned silence as I mechanically drove the car through the next town. Finally, Carrie just said something like, "I think we have our name."

Before you get too skeptical, I wasn't that guy. I didn't go looking for "signs" from God and often scoffed at those who put too much weight on circumstantial evidence of the providence of the Holy Spirit. The church sign didn't immediately confirm for me that the name was right, but it did open me up to explore why I liked it so much.

Jars show up all over Scripture because they were so prevalent in the culture. When Isaac needed a wife, the servant saw

Rachel with a jar heading to the watering hole. The Samaritan woman at the well was carrying a jar. When Jesus told the disciples how to find their place for the last supper, he told them to look for a man carrying a jar. Elijah had a widow fill as many jars as possible with miracle oil. And Paul said this:

> *But we have this treasure in jars of clay to show that the surpassing power belongs to God and not to us.*
> *– 2 Corinthians 4:7*

I told Carrie I was fascinated by the name because it spoke to me about the movement God had put on our hearts. My frustration came from seeing the same people showing up at the classes we were teaching. The. Same. People.

A group at our church had started calling themselves "The Lifers" because when I offered a curriculum called *Living in Grace* three different times, all of them had attended all three times. *Basic Discipleship*? Same. People. *Walking in the Spirit*? Same. People.

And guess what? When I finished a sermon, sometimes a person would come and ask me more questions because they weren't sure how to apply it in their lives. Same. People.

Even from that group who were Already Believers, only a smattering of them were regularly sharing their faith with those who were Not Yet believers. They were being filled up with knowledge, with Christian life skills, with the concepts of love, joy, peace, patience, kindness, goodness, faithfulness, gentleness, and self-control. What were they doing to empty themselves?

They were disciples, but were they disciple-makers?

I was frustrated by the lack of success. God used that as motivation to explore what it means for us to be filled by the Spirit of God, not to become good people, but to empty ourselves for the good of others.

Like a jar. A broken jar. A jar of clay where the treasures of God were held so that no one could deny the power came from Him and not from us.

The Jar, where we are filled to be emptied.

I was taught that success consisted of the "3 B's" in church: butts, bucks, and baptisms. No more. No more counting baptisms; I wanted to count baptizers. No more counting attendance; I wanted to count transformed lives. No more counting disciples; I wanted to count disciple-makers. I'd have to count money, but no more counting it for success; for that, I wanted to count blessings.

In my first book, *Rethink*, I shared how God helped me repent of (rethink) my frustration about my faith (allegiance). My hope is that you walked that journey with me and learned that our indignation about what the church has become can't be our motivation for change. We can't hate the church and love Jesus.

Maybe you think hate is a strong word, but I confess right here that the way I talked about the church—not the organization or the structure, not the teaching or the process, but the people—was hateful. What I said about those other pieces was worse. But God loves the church, even the members who aren't getting it. He loves them with unconditional love. Loves them. I cannot do otherwise and think to effect positive change in the Bride of Christ.

In the second book, *Follow*, we revisited what the Gospel—the Good News of Jesus Christ—really is. Not just a promise of eternal life in the Good Place and a chance to avoid the Bad Place, but a calling to become a citizen of the Kingdom of Heaven today. Right now. Eternity doesn't start when we die or when Jesus comes back. Eternity begins with the Kingdom of Heaven and Jesus told us the Kingdom is at hand. The moment we put our faith in Jesus, we enter.

My hope was to cure the frustration we feel about what it means to be saved and why transformation is as much a part of the Good News as salvation. He is our Savior, yes, but God is also our Lord. We aren't asked to obey so that God will approve; we are asked to follow so that God can be glorified.

We still have five frustrations left.

1. Church members
2. The Church
3. The world
4. Evangelism
5. Understanding the Spirit

This will be difficult territory because we have chosen to repent of (rethink) using our frustration as motivation and give our faith (allegiance) to the King of Heaven to help spread His influence in the world through love. We can't renege on those promises and then have a conversation about church members.

We may want to do just that. Heaven knows (literally) how hurtful some of them can be. Heaven knows (really knows) how little of the Good News many of them are spreading. Heaven knows (faithfully) that revival—though always available to us—seems so distant to us today despite all the polite talk about the need for it. Everyone wants everyone else to change, but no one wants to go first.

Frustrating, right?

But God wants our motivation to be love, not indignation. He wants us to reach deep inside us and find the courage to be what we wish those other church members would be. In other words, we need to become the disciples who learn how to make them disciple-makers. It isn't enough to complain, and it's downright sinful to isolate. Believe me, I fight both of those instincts often.

I want to quit. I want to give up. I want to let someone else make the effort.

But God…

Know why I feel so defeated? Because I'm not sure I can cause any real change. I would love to believe that my efforts can be fruitful. A part of me recognizes my inadequacy, and another part of me recognizes the resistance I will face. What difference can I really make?

Moses felt the same way standing in front of a burning bush. Five times, he asks God if He wouldn't mind finding someone else. After all, what about his inadequacy? What about the resistance? What difference could he really make?

But God…

I want to throw up my hands and let the enemy have them. Give them over, as Paul often says. Hm. I almost changed that last sentence because the truth is Paul doesn't "often" say it. In fact, he rarely said it and only after he had instructed the church to do everything in her power to bring them to rethink (repent of) the error of their ways. And then, he instructs them to restore their brothers and sisters to their allegiance (faith) before they succumb to the enemy.

> *For such a one, this punishment by the majority is enough, so you should rather turn to forgive and comfort him, or he may be overwhelmed by excessive sorrow. So, I beg you to reaffirm your love for him.*
> — *2 Corinthians 2:6-8*

If we have chosen to rethink and follow, we are still going to face the same frustrations with church members that we felt before. Going to them will not fill us up. Instead, it will drain us. We will try and fail, try and fail, try and fail, as we learn to empty ourselves for them. They can't fill us up with enough love, joy, peace, patience, kindness, goodness, faithfulness, gentleness, and self-control to make our fight worthwhile.

But God…

Once more into the breach, as Shakespeare wrote:

Pray for an open mind.
Listen for God's heart.
Let peace settle in your soul.
And rise up, Believer. Your King still reigns.

PART I

KNOW

TENSION:
Trust God or Trust the Church?

I remember being a teenager and running into this for the first time. A girlfriend of mine was jealous of a friendship I had with another girl. The second girl was more sister to me than potential romance, but that didn't matter to the one I was dating. I asked if she trusted me and got the famous line.

"I trust you, but I don't trust her."

But that didn't make sense to me. After all, if my sister-friend made advances on me, I would still have to respond, right? No matter how much I argued that she really meant she didn't trust me, she would not admit it. We broke up. After all, if she couldn't operate out of her trust in me regardless of my friend's intentions, she didn't really trust me.

I have to admit, though, that's how I feel about God and the Church sometimes. I believe wholeheartedly that God is willing to bring the Church back to her glory, remind her of her mission, and make her effective in our world today. A large part of me believes He is willing to revive the Church.

Before God dealt with my frustration, I wondered if He wanted to revive the Church. Was this what it meant to live in the end times? That God was still powerful enough, capable enough to bring life to the Church, but He no longer wanted to make the effort?

Sadly, I was projecting my frustration on God. Of course, He wants to revive the Church, just as He has countless times in the past. God can, He will, He wants to enlarge the Kingdom of God.

> *This is good, and it is pleasing in the sight of God our Savior, who desires all people to be saved and to come to the knowledge of the truth.*
>
> — *1 Timothy 2:3-4*

God is never motivated by frustration. He is always motivated by love. Even in the book of Revelation, He is acting out of His primary motivation. Despite all the calamity, the *purpose* of the vision He gave John is to drive people back to Him. It's not His fault that they don't.

> *The rest of mankind, who were not killed by these plagues, did not repent of the works of their hands nor give up worshiping demons and idols . . .*
>
> — *Revelation 9:21*

The plagues of the end times seem harsh, but John lets us know God's motivation for them. He wants them to repent of (rethink) their lives, stop following the things that hurt them, and put their faith in (give their allegiance to) Him.

But they don't.

Which is why, in my frustration, I would often think, "I trust God. I just don't trust the Church."

That sentence became a stronghold in my heart, soul, and mind, which sapped my strength to be what God was calling me to be. Even as I did everything I could to effect change as a church member, lay leader, church leader, and pastor, I didn't really think I could ever be successful.

But saying I trust God, but I don't trust the Church is similar to my girlfriend saying she doesn't trust my sister-friend. I must decide if I can operate out of trust in God instead of worrying about how the Church will act or respond.

I know I was wrong because I know God's will. In the end times, even the plagues won't turn people to the truth. But that won't stop God from trying again and again. Now, we have no guarantee that we live in those times despite the many well-meaning prophets who have told us otherwise. That means we must operate as if we still have time to reach the world. If God won't give up, and we are God's people, then what is our best response?

We can't sit idle, convinced that nothing can be done to revive the Church. We must fight against that stronghold by repenting of (rethinking) our intellectual position and putting our faith in (giving allegiance to) the only One Who has the power to bring the Church to life. Until we do that, we will devise plans but operate out of defeat. That's exactly how strongholds work.

But first, we should know what a stronghold is.

YOU HAD ONE JOB

The hardest part about reading the book of Job is understanding why God allowed the devil to do anything to Job in the first place. He's all-powerful and can dictate what He wishes to the enemy. Why allow him to steal, kill, and destroy in Job's life when Job was so obviously entrenched in his faithful obedience?

I know the arguments, and I know the ending. They don't give me much solace. I see how God protected Job through the process. I understand even the selection of Job as the target, though it seems to be Satan's idea, is actually controlled by God and even preferred by Him. Who else could have held to his faith through all that? I have been reminded that God blessed Job with twice what he had before going through it all, including having ten more children.

I'm not completely happy with it, though. I have four kids. If Elijah, Anna, Caitlin, and Nathan were suddenly torn from me in a horrific accident, having four more kids wouldn't cure my anger and grief at losing the first four, no matter what promises I had that I would see them in heaven.

When I let my guard down, though, the reason I struggle with the story is because of my own insecurity. Would I be able to keep my faith? Would I give up that much and still be devoted to God?

I used to think the answer was no, or at least that it was in doubt. No longer. I've been in a situation where I lost my reputation, my ministry, my home, half the family income, and the potential of never being able to answer God's call again. We also gained twice the monthly bills. I was forced to work the third shift in a physically demanding job in a body that had seen better than forty years just to afford an apartment in a more dangerous neighborhood.

What had I done to deserve such treatment? Nothing sinful. I was faithful to my wife, never beat my kids, worked crazy hours to promote our ministry, and shouldered many difficult decisions for my leaders. I made mistakes, yes. But I, like Job, could call up to God and say,

My eye has grown dim from vexation and all my members are like a shadow. The upright are appalled at this, and the innocent stirs himself up..."

— *Job 17:7-8a*

Helpful mentors and friends tried to explain it to me (like Job's friends), but most of the time, I felt like they weren't taking enough time to understand *me*. Their wisdom wasn't exactly wrong; just not, well, appropriate. I didn't need to consider if I was a "number one" or "number two" leader. I didn't need to justify myself again. I didn't need to revisit all my decisions.

I don't know that I could have pointed to what I needed except to know I needed God. Maybe, just maybe, that was how God was moving in Job's life. I've learned from my own experience that success—even spiritual success—can breed a necessity in us to remember we are dependent upon God.

Years have gone by, and I now see that God was trying to tell me to move on long before the nastiness happened. My wife knew before me, but I was blinded to it. I wanted my kids to graduate from a good school. I wanted to be successful in a place where so many other ministers had failed. I wanted to leave a legacy in that town.

God knew what I wanted but knew better what I needed. The suffering was necessary, in so many ways, for my growth. I never want to go through it again, but I am so glad God honored me by bringing me through it. I bet Job felt the same way.

One thing stood out to me, though, haunted me far longer than all the others. On that fateful night during a three-hour congregational meeting I'll never forget, one layperson stood up and shouted at me, snarling, spittle flying, murderous eyes, shouted as loudly as possible in front of all the people gathered, "Liar! Liar! God have mercy on your soul!"

My kids still tease me about it sometimes. But can I be honest? That declaration has hounded my ministry since. I'm constantly wondering if I've told the truth about everything I've said.

Have you ever noticed how addicts who are recovering are suddenly extra careful not to lie? They can't tell a story without ruining it by being as exact as possible with the facts.

"I was at Wal-Mart the other night . . . No, it wasn't night. It was late evening, and it was Tuesday. No,

Wednesday because it was right before my third AA meeting. I was with a friend. Well, he's not really a friend. We got to meetings together sometimes…"

That's been me in ministry. Why? Because I don't want that layperson to be right. Ever. And as for God having mercy on my soul? I struggle sometimes with believing my worth to do things like lead a church, write a book, and talk about Jesus. Even if I don't think about it very often anymore, that one declaration has become a loop track that occasionally starts playing on repeat in my head. When it does, my decision-making becomes tentative, my doubts get the better of me, and if things don't go well, I want to shoulder all the blame.

Woe on my conscience if someone thinks I said something I didn't, and woe on the person who confronts me about something I know I didn't do.

I believe this kind of loop track is called a stronghold in the Bible. Paul mentions it in his last letter to the Corinthians as he is defending his ministry (hmm. Like I find myself doing every time that track starts playing…).

For though we walk in the flesh, we are not waging war according to the flesh. For the weapons of our warfare are not of the flesh but have divine power to destroy strongholds. We destroy arguments and every lofty opinion raised against the knowledge of God and take every thought captive to obey Christ…

— 2 Corinthians 10:3-5

19

The apostle was being accused of "walking in the flesh" of satisfying his own ambitions and dreams. He wanted them to know he was above that; his motivation was the love of Christ, and his warfare was not even with them as they mocked and doubted him. No, the battle was happening on a completely different level.

He knew he was engaged in a spiritual battle, fought against an enemy that looks for opportunities to control our thought life. If we allow that, this enemy knows he can control us even if we are trying to live by the Spirit. Paul combats the complaints by deciding to wage war on the real foe.

First, he admits that as a human being, he does sometimes walk in the flesh. He knows the struggle of living by the Spirit and admits his faults. I'm still learning how to do this consistently. Sometimes, I'm not willing to say I'm wrong. But I find more often, I've become overly judgmental about my actions and decisions. I don't want to say I'm getting it right. The loop track still messes with me even as I explain how to relieve myself from it!

After this admission, he points to where the real war is. God's divine power can destroy strongholds, cure us of those loop tracks, and renew our minds. Paul confesses he doesn't have the power himself by pointing to the only Power that works.

> *His divine power has granted to us all things pertaining to life and godliness through the knowledge of Him who called us to His own glory and excellence…*
>
> *— 2 Peter 1:3*

He then says that Power helps them "destroy arguments and every lofty opinion raised against the knowledge of God." This phrasing gives us insight into the purpose of the strongholds. They are arguments against what God would have us know. They are high-sounding opinions that seem right but are still against what God says. The best lies are 90% true, after all.

DISTINGUISHING TRUTH

What can we do to combat those right-sounding critiques that have taken residence in our minds? *I have lied before and will lie again. Am I a liar? I do need God to have mercy on my soul. Were they right?* How can we see through to the knowledge that God wants us to have? We "…take every thought captive to obey Christ."

> *So Jesus said to the Jews who had believed Him, "If you abide in My word, you are truly My disciples, and you will know the truth, and the truth will set you free."*
> — *John 8:31-32*

Notice Jesus says this to His own people who already believe in Him. This isn't a message for doubters, for people riding on the fence. He's been teaching at the festival and these people have gathered around Him because they have believed He may truly be the Messiah. This teaching *is* true for Not Yet Believers, but we sometimes forget it is also true for Already Believers.

21

If Jesus is "the way, the *truth*, and the life" (John 14:6, emphasis mine), then this passage can deepen our understanding of Paul's teaching. When we take every thought captive for Christ, we are deciding that we are going to trust Jesus for what is true and what is not.

When I hear that loop track, I don't have to listen to it. God does not see me as a liar, and my soul is not in jeopardy because of the work of Christ on the cross and in the resurrection. I may not yet be free of it, but I can at least recognize the lies in it. How can I know they are lies? By using the weapon God gave me to discover the truth: Jesus.

As the lies uttered that day start playing in a loop in my head, I defeat that stronghold by taking captive every thought for Jesus. I can only do this if I *know* Jesus. I can only know Jesus if I discover all I can about Him in the Word.

Paul understood how to help his young protégé Timothy figure this out. Timothy had what I believe is a stronghold in his life. He thought he was too young and didn't know enough to lead people in the church. To combat that, Paul reminded him how strongholds are defeated. He doesn't say, "You're not really that young, Timothy, don't worry about it." That would discount reality and do no good for his pupil. Instead, Paul calls Timothy his child several times in the same letter.

Paul doesn't excuse the issue. He teaches him to overcome it. Before he said, "Let no one despise you for your youth..." (1 Timothy 4:12), he had a message for his acolyte:

Have nothing to do with irreverent, silly myths. Rather train yourself for godliness; for while bodily training is of some value, godliness is of value in every way, as it holds promise for the present life and also for the life to come.
— *1 Timothy 4:7-8*

He goes on to say Timothy can trust this because it is the reason they work so hard to set their hope on our Savior and that we should command and teach those things to others. Combatting the stronghold of "I'm too young or too unqualified" required renewing his devotion to training himself for godliness.

Been thinking for a long time about the word "godliness." I did a word study one time and realized how often it was used in a list of other words. And if it is included in a list, it must mean something a little different than the things on the list.

Keeping this in mind, I discovered godliness can't exactly mean power, life, faith, virtue, knowledge, self-control, brotherly love, agape love, holiness, contentment, righteousness, endurance, or gentleness (Check out 1 & 2 Timothy 2 Peter 1:3-8, 2 Peter 3:11, Acts 3:12).

So what is it? The word comes from the Greek root, *eusebeia*, and can best be expressed as "to worship well" to have a sense of piety. That last word is worth five dollars. Here's the fifty-cent version: Godliness is to naturally express devotion to God.

Don't miss this, brothers and sisters. For Timothy to break himself from his stronghold, he needed to train himself in such a way that he naturally expressed his devotion to God. After all, God is the One who called him! God is the one he can trust to tell the truth!

How did Paul tell Timothy to do that? How can we do that today?

BECOMING AN EXPRESSION OF GOD

In Paul's second letter to Timothy, he gives a reminder of how his young helper was taught to follow God. We always land on 2 Timothy 3:16, and we will, but don't miss what comes before that passage. Listen to Paul:

> *You, however, have followed my teaching, my conduct, my aim in life, my faith, my patience, my love, my stead-fastness, my persecutions and sufferings . . . yet from them all the Lord rescued me.*
>
> — *2 Timothy 3:10-11*

Do you see it? Of course Paul included his teachings (that leads us to the 3:16 passage in a minute). Do you see what else he included?

- **MY CONDUCT.** Paul didn't just teach Timothy how to behave; he behaved that way as an example. The younger had watched; the older lived it out.

- **MY AIM IN LIFE.** Not only how Paul lived, Timothy saw the *reason* Paul lived that way. The purpose was as important as the example.
- **MY FAITH.** The apostle had given his allegiance to Jesus in such a way that he could expect Timothy to know it without questioning it.
- **MY PATIENCE, LOVE, STEADFASTNESS.** I include all these together because I believe they prepare Timothy for what Paul's about to share. Without patience, love, and perseverance, Paul could not have handled…
- **MY PERSECUTIONS AND SUFFERINGS**. Interesting, isn't it, that Paul includes the bad times as well as the good things in the reminder? Something about them would teach Timothy an important lesson: the Lord had rescued Paul from them all!

Paul was saying, "You and I have been *talmidim* (disciples) together to the greatest Rabbi ever, the One Messiah Who died for us and rose again, Who taught us all we need to know, Who strengthens us through the Holy Spirit to do what we must do. I am further along than you, though, so watch me, be an imitator of me, as I imitate Him (1 Corinthians 11:1)."

Then Paul says, "But as for you, continue in what you have learned and have firmly believed…" (2 Timothy 3:14) before he goes on to say what we so often quote out of context. The Word is important, yes, but in the context of disciple-making…

All Scripture is God-breathed and profitable for teaching, for reproof, for correction, and for training in righteousness, that the man of God may be complete, equipped for every good work.

— 2 Timothy 3:16-17

The rescue comes partly from knowing the Word and understanding the character of the Father, the work of the Son, and the power of the Holy Spirit to help us love as God intended. Only from the Word can we see the truth of these important lessons. In fact, Paul is very particular about his list of results from our study. He says it is profitable for . . .

- **Teaching.** Showing us what is true.
- **Reproof.** Showing us where we believed the lies and acted on them.
- **Correction.** Showing us what it looks like to do it right.
- **Training in righteousness.** Giving us opportunity to do it better the next time.

These are all important steps, but do you notice what they require? *Acting* on what has been learned. Too often, we look at this passage and say, "See, this is why we should study the Word!" When in reality, this passage says, "See, this is how we should follow Jesus!" And if we're going to follow Jesus this way, wouldn't it be great if we had some people around us who were further along than we are? That way, we can know God well enough to trust Him to help us become what He is making us so we can live it out for others as an example to follow.

That should sound familiar if you've read my first two books, *Rethink* and *Follow*.

Know. Be. Live.

BREAKING THIS STRONGHOLD

I'm hoping this teaching speaks to parts of your life this book doesn't cover. You may have strongholds in your life and didn't realize what they were. These loop tracks were started by your parents, your siblings, your schoolmates, your business partners, your fellow employees, your church, yourself (really, they were started by the enemy), and they sound something like…

You should be ashamed.
You aren't worth it.
You'll never amount to anything.
You've done too many bad things for God to still love you.
You haven't done enough for God to love you yet.
You've done too much for *anyone* to love you.
You'll always be single.
Your marriage will always be unhappy.
You don't count.
You can't stop.

And a thousand others like it. My hope is that this begins to show you the way to healing in that area of your life. Take captive every thought for Christ and recognize the lies you were told. I mean this. They are lies.

You are guilty, but not shameful. You've done wrong things; you are not the wrong sort of person. Tell the enemy that's a lie.

God so loved *you* that He sent His Son to die for you. You're worth it. Tell the enemy that's the truth.

You are a child of the King. You are already a co-heir with Christ, and that amounts to everything. Tell the enemy about your Father.

No one is so far in the darkness that a flicker of light can't dispel it. You are not hopelessly lost as long as Jesus sits on the throne. Tell the enemy that Jesus is your hope.

Your efforts never could win the love God already has for you. If you have to earn it, it's not really love but approval. Tell the enemy God's love isn't in question.

Everyone deserves to be loved. You do, too. God says so!

Being single isn't a prison sentence. Be who God made you to be, and learn to be content. That's usually when the right one comes along, anyway.

God made marriage before He made the church. He cares about your marriage too much to turn His back on it. What can He teach you to improve it?

You matter to God. You matter to people. You matter.

And yes, you can. Stop, that is. Maybe not by yourself, but it can be done. As a former alcoholic, I'm living proof.

BACK IN FOCUS

I wish I could go on from here to address every stronghold the enemy may have put in your mind, but that's beyond the scope of this book. Maybe after this journey is done, that will be our new journey together. For now, though, we're focused on one stronghold in particular.

The stronghold of unbelief in God's ability to revive the church.

The enemy has convinced many of us that God either won't or can't reach enough of the Christian people of today to effect the changes necessary. We cite anecdotal evidence to prove it. We look at the statistics gathered by our well-meaning pollster brethren. We do our own informal questionnaire with other believers we consider "awake," and we come to one conclusion:

We can trust God, but we can't trust the Church.

As if that is new today. As if our frustration with the church isn't literally written into the pages of the New Testament. As if Paul, James, Peter, John, and Jude were never frustrated…

> *Therefore, you have no excuse, O man, every one of you who judges. For in passing judgment on another, you condemn yourself because you, the judge, practice the very same things.*
>
> *— Romans 2:1*

But I, brothers, could not address you as spiritual people but as people of the flesh, as infants in Christ.

— 1 Corinthians 3:1

For if someone comes and proclaims another Jesus than the One we proclaimed, or if you receive a different Spirit from the One you received, or if you accept a different gospel from the one you accepted, you put up with it readily enough.

— 2 Corinthians 11:4

You were running well. Who hindered you from obeying the truth?

— Galatians 5:7

For if we go on sinning deliberately after receiving the knowledge of the truth, there no longer remains a sacrifice for sins…

— Hebrews 10:26

What causes quarrels and what causes fights among you? Is it not this: that your passions are at war within you?

— James 4:1

But false prophets also arose among the people, just as there will be false teachers among you . . .

— 2 Peter 2:1a

I have written something to the church, but Diotrephes, who likes to put himself first, does not acknowledge our authority.

— 3 John 9

They said to you, "In the last times, there will be scoffers, following their own ungodly passions."

— Jude 18

Let's not pretend this is new for the Church. We have never been trustworthy. Praise Jesus the survival of the Good News was never contingent upon a trustworthy Church. Our faith was always built on a trustworthy God.

Let's walk through what Paul suggests when he tells us how to battle against strongholds. We need to pull all this together and see it for the process it is. Process, not event, that starts with this phrase: But God....

1. **Admit we walk in the flesh.** We fall sometimes, screw up most days, make bad decisions. We let people down, say the wrong thing, hurt people's feelings. We miss a doctrinal point, preach a shallow Gospel, and carry a theological blindspot. Let's all confess that we are sometimes the problem.

2. **Focus our efforts on where the battle is taking place.** Don't let the enemy fool you. The sanctuary isn't the battleground. Neither is the elder's meeting.

Or the small group. Or the fellowship hall. The battle is spiritual and must take place in spiritual territory.

3. **Rely on the only Power that can destroy this thinking.** The Spirit of God is the only one who knows fully the Mind of God, not us (1 Corinthians 2:11), and is the only Power that wins the war.

4. **Destroy that argument with repentance (rethinking) and faith (allegiance).** Declare to God that you are ready to rethink (repent of) your view of the church and put your faith (allegiance) in Jesus to bring about the changes necessary.

WHOSE JOB IS IT, ANYWAY?

When I was about ten, a buddy and I were feeling pretty down about having no money. When you're ten and you have a single mom, money is not exactly growing on trees (as Mom would say). What could we do?

My friend had a great idea. We took some brooms and a rake out through his backyard, across an alley, and through the parking lot of the hardware store. Walking inside, we asked to see the owner. Thinking back now, I'm surprised the owner even came out to talk with us.

We told him we had noticed that his parking lot was filthy. We would be willing to clean it if he would pay us two dollars an hour. To our excitement, he agreed. We went outside, eager to put in the work. We swept and raked and sweat and dumped and piled like we had families at home depending on that money.

About an hour into it, the owner came out to check on us. Boy, was he mad. See, we had been sweeping up all the gravel in his parking lot and throwing it in a grassy area by the dumpster. We'd done a great job so far. We were just doing the wrong job. He paid us for our hour and sent us packing.

I don't know if he ever got all the little stones out of that grassy area.

This is my fear for those who love Jesus but are frustrated with the church. We'll take that eagerness to work at fixing the Church but try to clear out all the gravel instead of picking up the real trash. If we do, we can pat ourselves on the back for doing such a great job. We'll just be doing the wrong job.

What follows is a simple way to keep in mind our part in God's Kingdom plan. It isn't perfect, and it isn't complete, but it sets us in the right direction as we prepare to break the stronghold in our minds about the church.

- **The Father's job is to judge.** We don't have the power or the right to condemn anyone. God will do that at the appropriate time. He's the only one qualified to do it because He's the only one who perfectly understands righteousness. Since we can't fix the church by condemning everyone, let's leave that to God. He does many other things, but this one thing He keeps for Himself.

- **The Holy Spirit's job is to convict.** Of course, the Spirit does many other things, but we sometimes forget that Jesus told us the Spirit will convict the world of sin, righteousness, and judgment (John 16:8). Sometimes, we try to take His place by making others feel convicted about what we see as their sin. Since we can't fix the church by convicting people of their wrongdoing, let's leave that to God. The Holy Spirit does many things, but this one thing He keeps for Himself.

- **The Son's job is to save.** We also don't have the power or the right to save anyone. Jesus does that through His finished work (sinless life, introduction of the Kingdom, death, burial, and resurrection). He's the only one qualified to do it because He's the only one Who could pay the price of justification. Since we can't fix the Church by saving people, let's leave that to God. He does many other things, but this one thing Jesus keeps for Himself.

- **Our job is to love.** Yes, God is love. I'm not saying the Father, Son, and Holy Spirit don't love. What I'm saying is this is our one true job. To love God enough to understand His grace and truth leads us to repent (rethink) and give Him our allegiance (faith) and to love others enough to share that grace and truth with the people around us. To be filled to be emptied. To make them disciples who make disciples.

That's why the Sermon on the Mount is littered with teaching that leads to love. Don't hate your brother—that's murder, and that's not loving to others. Don't look at others lustfully—that's adultery, and that's not loving to your spouse, and it objectifies the other person. Love your enemies—an impossibility unless God is enabling us. Love is the way we live and move in the business of the Kingdom.

We can't condemn anyone, convict anyone, or save anyone. All we can do is love everyone (with godly love) and let the Father, Son, and Holy Spirit do His work in them.

We can't fix the church.

But God…

TEACHING:
Reaching the Middles

Ever had a big decision you couldn't make in a moment? Something up to you and nobody else, but you knew it would change everything for everyone? That kind of decision chases sleep away. Drives up anxiety. Amps up the pressure.

Leaving our wonderful church was that kind of decision. I look back and believe with all my heart that we did our best to avoid friction in the process. We still said and did things we shouldn't have. Some of that came from the stress of the decision-making process. One thing I can tell you is that this kind of decision improves your prayer life. Maybe we did okay with our prayer time before God called us to plant, but afterward, we ramped up. Had to. We knew God was the only one supplying answers.

I wonder if Jesus felt the same way when He disappeared one evening. Matthew says He called the twelve to Him. Mark says He went up on a mountain and called the twelve to Him. Luke gives us a little different take…

In these days He (Jesus) went out to the mountain to pray, and all night continued in prayer to God. And when day came, He called His disciples and chose from them twelve whom He named apostles…

Luke 6:12-13

A sleepless night spent communicating with His Father. This decision was extraordinary. The Son and the Father, hashing out the disciples available to Him. I know, I know, it's crazy and seems a bit blasphemous. But I think God was showing us the humanity of Jesus here. He wanted to make the right decision because what was coming next was going to be difficult. Not just life-changing; world-changing.

Apostolos is a Greek word that means, at its root, messenger. Yet it means so much more. Envoy. Ambassador. The one entrusted to deliver the message of the one who sent them. In this case, Jesus, the Messiah, the Anointed One, is sending. The twelve selected to lead this next phase of the ministry had to be right.

Don't get me wrong. I don't think the decision was left to chance, and I don't think Jesus could have been wrong about this. Son of God, right? This just tells us how important a calling is. Jesus, the Son of God, spoke with God the Father *all night* before deciding which twelve would carry His message.

Those twelve had to be humbled, taught, and prepared for what was coming. They had to willingly follow Jesus and watch everything He did.

And He appointed twelve (whom He also named apostles)
so they might be with Him, and He might send them out
to preach and have authority to cast out demons.
                                    — Mark 3:14-15

Not just preach or do the miracle stuff; they were chosen to be with Him. In approximately three years, they would be asked to shoulder the second greatest burden of mankind after their Rabbi Jesus shouldered the first greatest. After Jesus shouldered the sins of mankind, the Gospel would be theirs to share first.

Even as Jesus chose His twelve, though, He was also bringing light to the rest of the disciples. They, too, would be called upon to spread the message. In Matthew 10, Jesus sends the twelve out for the first time by themselves. In Luke 10, Jesus sends out seventy-two. The Apostles were sent out the first time to proclaim, "The Kingdom of Heaven is at hand." The second group, which probably included the Apostles? They were sent out to proclaim, "The Kingdom of Heaven has come near you!"

I'm not saying that makes all of them Apostles, but it does, in a way, mean that each disciple has an apostolic duty. Think about it. Jesus spent all night praying to select the first twelve—they were that important—but in no time at all sent a larger group to preach the same thing.

Why do I bring this up?

Because in this volume we are addressing our frustration with the members of the Church. If we repent of (rethink) our perspective on the Church and put our faith in (give allegiance

39

to) Jesus, then we are also being asked to *be with Jesus* so that we can help others see what it looks like to, well, be with Jesus. As we noted earlier, Paul understood his example was nearly as important as the doctrine he was teaching.

> *Be imitators of me, as I am of Christ.*
> — *1 Corinthians 11:1*

The importance of our repentance (rethinking) and faith (allegiance) is that we are put in a position to be an example (disciple-maker) to the rest of the church. Once we've gained a heavenly perspective, we are ready to look at the average church member fairly, clearly, and humbly.

This is important. Know why?

BECAUSE OUR PERSPECTIVE MATTERS

If we aren't careful, we will slip into one of two camps. Either we will go back to what we knew (I'm changing the church for me) or submit to the stronghold (nothing can change the church). Either one will render us unfruitful and ineffective in our faith (more on this later). To avoid that, we must be honest about where the church is today as we remember that we make disciples for God's sake, not for our own.

Okay. Deep breath. Let's dive in.

One of the things we still fight in our church culture is the propensity to "let the clergy do it." Evangelism? That's the pastor's job. Disciple-making? That's the pastor's job. Many church people are content to let the professional Christians do all the spiritual heavy lifting. And here's the thing: to some extent, it's not their fault.

They've been given a selfish version of the Gospel where their salvation and their growth into a better version of themselves is the goal. We talked in the second volume, *Follow*, about two distortions of the Gospel. Each of them fundamentally changes our understanding of the mission of the church.

The Grace-Only Gospel focuses on our salvation as the finish line. We want to see everyone forgiven for their sins, so we introduce to them the sacrifice Jesus made. We focus on the death and resurrection of Jesus and do our best to get them to say the prayer, ask Jesus into their hearts, and get baptized. Once this decision is made, they have eternal life. The mission of this Gospel, then, is to get them into heaven.

The Truth-Only Gospel focuses on our behavior. Yes, yes, we are saved still by the sacrifice of Jesus and a decision must be made. But the important thing is to closely mimic the life of Jesus as we try to become holier and holier through our lives. Some believe "backsliding" into a life of sin can lead to the loss of salvation. Others believe they can't lose their salvation, but they can lose the blessing. The mission of this Gospel is to make people good until they get to heaven.

John tells us in the first chapter of his Gospel that Jesus is full of grace *and* truth. The point of the Gospel of Jesus Christ is to advance the Kingdom of God by setting more and more of the captives free to become followers of the King. This is the mission of God: to reclaim His Kingdom among the people. That's why I settled on this summary of the Gospel . . .

The Kingdom of Heaven is reclaiming earth through the life, death, and resurrection of Jesus Christ of Nazareth, God's only Son. We who repent of our sins and give allegiance to King Jesus are forgiven and empowered by the Holy Spirit to spread His influence and boldly follow Him.

This Grace-and-Truth Gospel returns the church to the mission given to us by God, which is no different than what Jesus gave to the Apostles and the disciples. We are to proclaim that the Kingdom of Heaven is at hand to as many as will listen.

We are to proclaim. Every one of us.

Not just the pastors and priests, ministers and deacons, elders and lay leaders.

You. Me. We.

Maybe you think this is too small a place to start. The church is in such dire straits. How can one person returning to the mission change anything? The magnitude of it is frustrating. Even more frustrating is the number of believers who are not aware of or willing to engage in the mission. How can we make a difference?

That's the stronghold in our church today. We have bought into the lie that it takes a megachurch to make a difference. I can prove it by asking one more question.

How can twelve men so revolutionize the world that Christianity would become such a culture-altering force in just 300 years?

The answer isn't the genius of the twelve men. It's the Holy Spirit guiding them into the mission. The same Holy Spirit is available today. God not only can revive the church today; He *wants* to revive it. His desire is that all people be saved (1 Timothy 2:4).

Before we go any further, we must decide whether or not to believe this. I know you're frustrated. Me, too. But remember what we learned together in *Rethink*.

Wait. Pray. Respond under God's authority.

Pray, brother; pray, sister. Pray that God enlightens you to become one of the dozens He is sending to revive the church. Not because you're special but because He is powerful.

Do you believe God is just as frustrated by the state of the Church as you are? Do you believe He wants to bring true revival to as many of the members of the Church as possible? Do you believe it has to start somewhere, so it might as well be you? Can you trust Him, even if you can't trust the Church?

Then, learn this first lesson.

Disciple-making is not for you.

I know this is a confusing way to start the discussion, but I believe this sentence creates a new path for the church. Those who are Not Yet believers, bear with us as we have some insider conversation. Keep reading, though, because you might get an explanation for some of your bad experiences with church people.

Already Believers, this will do the same for you and might help you understand even more. I'm not labeling anyone—and you should be careful, too—but I was taught to look for a pattern and found it to be true. Those who Already Believe can be broken into three groups. Please let me explain.

My professor in college once taught that in any church, ten percent of the people gathering each Sunday will not let themselves be discipled no matter what the pastor does. This breaks my heart, but I have seen its truth. The figure may be off and may change in size from one congregation to another, but the statement is still valid. Each person fending off faith in our churches has personal reasons, but we can name some, can't we?

Church is a social club. Church is a comfort. Church is something to scratch off my spiritual to-do list. Church is expected. Church gets me business. Church is where I have power. Church makes me feel saved.

We'll call them the Others. These people drain a pastor. They tend to need more support, tend to be less satisfied, and tend to be the main source of complaints. The Others are there for what the Church can do for them.

Then, my professor taught that in any church, twenty percent are Type-A go-getters who reach for disciple-making no matter what form the pastor gives it. Drop them in a room with a Bible and leave. In thirty minutes, some form of disciple-making is happening. We'll call them Type-A's.

These people excite a pastor. They want to know what a disciple is, what a disciple does, how a disciple makes more disciples. They are the energy a pastor needs to feel like the work is not in vain. To Type-A's, the church is a university, an opportunity to serve, a hospital, and the base of operations; the church is where to bring people looking for Jesus.

Most pastors spend time with one of these two groups. We don't set out to let them monopolize our ministry, but they often do. While seventy percent of our congregation finds its own way, we either vainly reach out to the Others or give our egos a boost with the Type-A's.

I want to reach everyone, so sometimes I focus on the Others to the exclusion of everyone else. When that becomes unbearable, I fall back on the Type-A's who would get it if I just left them alone. I want to feel successful, so sometimes, I focus on the self-starters to the exclusion of everyone else. When that becomes unsatisfying (or worse, too satisfying), I bypass the middle and reach for the Others again.

As I pondered this truth in myself, the professor said the 70% in the middle were the ones he was teaching us to reach. The ones who haven't joined either of the first two groups but are wondering why they are asked to attend church each week. They go because they know it's good for them, but they don't

45

think they can really be disciples of Jesus. The notion seems too lofty or too difficult or too saintly for someone like them. But they dream of it a little.

THE MIDDLES

For years, we've diagnosed the disease killing the effectiveness of the Western church today. At some point, the Church forgot her mission to go and make disciples. Hundreds of books have been published on the subject. Movements started. Lives changed, and hearts transformed. People are taking this seriously, and because of it, I believe the Church is positioning for revival, not defeat.

Seeing the work done by so many great leaders, I have a different perspective on all the church closings and the drop in attendance since the pandemic. What we see is pruning, not diminishing. God is consolidating the Church to make her more dynamic. He is removing His blessing from congregations more consumed with comfort and less consumed with mission. This is harsh, I know, and it hurts my heart to say it. In many places today, across all denominational lines, churches are refusing to follow great leaders whose only crime is rearranging the furniture in the House of God to appeal to the culture of today.

"The eye is the lamp of the body. So, if your eye is healthy, your whole body will be full of light, but if your eye is

bad, your whole body will be full of darkness. If then the light in you is darkness, how great is that darkness!"
                                        — Jesus in Matthew 6:22-23

Jesus tells us we can choose our perspective, and that choice will lead us to light or to darkness. Jesus asks me to choose the light. For so long, in my frustration, I saw only darkness. Now that I have repented of (rethought) my position and put my faith (allegiance) in Him to help me complete the mission, I see the beautiful life of the Church ready to set fire to the world. Others who have made their religion more churchianity than Christianity are truly out there—I see them—but I choose to focus on the ones who are getting back to the mission.

When I do, however, I see movements focusing on the Type-A twenty percent who want to get it. I read those books and even I am discouraged about my ability to follow. Sell my house and move to the inner city. Create 90% participation in small groups in my church. Leave my ministry and head to Africa. Be fearless, undaunted, faith-filled, risk-loving, radical, and crazy. Lead like Jesus. Live like Luke would mention my name in Acts if he were writing today. I am challenged by them but left speechless, aimless. I don't know how to follow what they are portraying.

I'm part of the middle group. I'm one of the 70%.

I have some Type-A in me, but I also have some Type-ADD. I want to be fearless, but my greatest fear is to be exposed as a fraud in my faith. I am an introvert in an extrovert's world. Sometimes, I wonder if I'm an introvert in an extrovert's religion. I'm administratively challenged, and my ambitions ebb and flow. And I'm a pastor!

Years after my professor sparked this realization in me, I was leading a new church and trying to discover how to crack the code for discipling the Middle Group. Not the stars of the church. Just people. I studied and came up with some ideas over the years, but not until recently did all the pieces fit into place. I think the best way to start is with a fence.

WE NEED FENCES

One of my favorite analogies is learning to play in the yard. When we were little, our parents turned us loose in the backyard. They let us do mostly what we wanted so long as we didn't go outside the fence without permission. If a ball went over, we didn't have the right to chase it. If a friend came over, we didn't have the right to jump the fence and go somewhere with them. That boundary kept us safe and honest while letting us explore our imaginations.

In the same way, disciple-making needs fences. Here are mine:

1. **The disciple-making process must be biblically accurate.** I can't decide what it means to be a disciple. What I teach must be backed up by Scripture so that I can identify God's fence. It wasn't put there to restrain me but to protect me.

2. **The disciple-making process must be aimed at the Middle Group.** It's okay to make a process for the go-getters, but that's not the focus God has given me. I can't chase the ball over the fence.

3. **The disciple-making process must avoid doctrinal controversies.** Since we are talking about how to live out our faith after salvation, much of this is avoided anyway. The controversies that remain are not central to the faith, and we can make disciples together while agreeing to disagree. I can't hop the fence to be with friends.

4. **The disciple-making process must teach people how to think, not what to think.** We don't need lemmings; we need lifers. I don't want anyone to follow me. I want them to follow Jesus in the way God shows them.

5. **The disciple-making process must be progressive as a plan but flexible as a path.** We can provide guidance while allowing individual freedom. Let people play inside the fence without dictating what that play must look like. I'm trying to describe an organic system, not a program.

By staying true to these guidelines, I keep myself from creating heresy while avoiding doctrinal controversy. I aim people away from me and toward Jesus. I help Middles realize that disciple-making is attainable and expected while leaving room for their personalities. In this way, we help God cast the net wide to serve one more, reach one more, teach one more, and help one more grow in Christ.

WHAT IS TRUE ACROSS DENOMINATIONS?

I was starting a new ministry in Northern Indiana. Given the chance to seek a new path toward congregational health, I plunged back into my thoughts and notes about fulfilling the mission. If we could make disciples who make disciples of the Middle Group there, we could make an impact for the Kingdom of God in that region.

For the first time in my life, I started the ministry teaching about prayer. Prayer, after all, is universal in the faith. As I taught and formed a prayer team and considered what God was showing me, I realized I needed to do a series on disciple-making for them. Though we agreed on our doctrine, I saw it as an opportunity to teach past our version of church and speak into the hearts of the congregation what they could share with the Methodists and Brethren down the street.

I asked the question, "What is true no matter what I think about baptism, spiritual gifts, communion (Eucharist), end times, musical leanings, or any other controversial issue in the church?"

All those topics are important, and we should not avoid them. We should discuss them with other believers even if we disagree. However, if we spend all our time on disagreements, we lose the power in the intersection of our faith. My goal was to create a disciple-making process that could be used regardless of a person's denominational experience. What is true no matter what part of the body resonates with me?

We are all called to:

The Great Commission . . .
    . . . using the Great Commandments . . .
    . . . to spread the Good News of Jesus Christ.

These three ideas are central to every church, regardless of the doctrine surrounding them. What can we teach that leads people to remember these things? More importantly, what can we teach the Middles that will encourage them to participate and enliven them to their part in the spiritual battle unfolding around us? What makes Christians want to fulfill the mission God gave us?

> *"**As you go**, therefore, make disciples of all the nations [help the people to learn of Me, believe in Me, and obey My words], baptizing them in the name of the Father and of the Son and of the Holy Spirit, teaching them to observe everything that I have commanded you . . ."*
>   *— Matthew 28:19-20a,*
>   *Amplified Bible, emphasis mine*

I started thinking about this passage and how the verb choice at the very beginning makes all the difference for the Middles. Most English versions of this passage start out "Go, therefore…' So often, we prompt, prod, and provoke people to go out and fulfill the mission of Jesus. I think Type-A's need to hear that because the challenge lights them on fire.

But not the Middles. Middles start asking, "Where would I go? What about the life I've built? What about my family and friends and job?" I believe teachers often misinterpret these questions. They double down and tell Middles if they really loved Jesus, none of that would matter. Maybe some of them need to hear that, but I think more often, the Middle is really asking, "How does that square with my responsibilities? Doesn't Jesus also want me to be responsible?"

Made to feel guilty, the Middle is left with diametrically opposed concepts of what it means to follow Jesus. On the one hand, a true follower will uphold the obligations of life. On the other hand, a true follower will drop all obligations for a risk-centered life. This teaching doesn't always cause Middles to consider if they are effective for the Kingdom. Sometimes, it causes them to question the validity of the faith. How can it be both?

But it can! All we need to recognize is the difference between "Go" and "As you go," and the dilemma is cleared up. Jesus isn't telling everyone to be a missionary to some foreign place (Africa or another city or a group of people the Middle doesn't know). He's telling everyone to be a missionary where He plants them (unless He sends them).

More to teach here, right? That'll come later. Right now, I want to stick with the Middles, who just realized maybe disciple-making is for them, after all. Okay, so to be on mission is to take Jesus with them. How do they know they are on mission? By the Great Commandments.

> *"… 'Hear, O Israel, the Lord our God is one Lord; and you shall love the Lord your God with all your heart, and with all your soul (life), and with all your mind (thought, understanding), and with all your strength.' This is the second: 'You shall [unselfishly] love your neighbor as your-self.' There is no other commandment greater than these."*
> — *Mark 12:29-31, Amplified Bible*

The mission is to love God and love people as we love our-selves. Sometimes we get confused here. We start thinking to be on mission is to pray, to read, to be in a small group, to join a church, to serve in the body, to finish whatever task list is created for us. Even when the teacher is not confused, the Middles are.

"Wait. Not only do I have to go somewhere uncomfortable and shirk all my obligations, but I also need to fill my time with this list of things? When am I going to fit them in?"

Once again, the penchant for on-fire, Type-A, extrovert teachers is to misinterpret the concern. They answer the Middle in the same way as before: if you love Jesus, you will do these things. This assumes the Middle is one of the Others, the bottom ten-percenters. This assumes the Middle doesn't have enough faith, enough drive, enough love for Jesus. Sometimes, this is the case because the Middle is drifting down toward the Others and needs to wake up.

Often, though, this is a why question, not a how question. Why do we do these things? The Middle wants proof these things are important enough to disrupt the obligations they already have. When the list becomes the mission, the list is burdensome.

The list isn't the mission. Loving God and loving people is the mission. The list is a collection of tools in the toolbox to help the mission succeed. I pray because my communication with God shows, builds, and deepens my love for God. I read because the more I know God, the greater my love for Him. I'm in a small group to learn how to love the household of faith and let them love me, and I am driven to do that by my love for God. And so on. I use these things to develop the greatest love I can have for God and for people and for me.

What is the greatest expression of that love?

For I passed on to you as of first importance what I also received, that Christ died for our sins according to [that which] the Scriptures [foretold], and that He was buried, and that He was [bodily] raised on the third day according to [that which] the Scriptures [foretold] . . ."
— *1 Corinthians 15:3-4, Amplified Bible*

Sharing the Good News of Jesus Christ.

We love people when we teach them how to be good parents or, spouses or, neighbors or employees. We love them when we teach them how to pray, or study the Bible, or make the most of church. We love them when we serve them during hurricanes, floods, mass shootings, and other disasters. We love them when we offer aid in everyday events—opening doors, carrying heavy stuff, mowing lawns, raking leaves. We love them when we provide support and supplies for their daily needs—food pantries, back-to-school events, addiction counseling, and grief recovery workshops.

But the greatest love we can show them is The Way to eternal glory through the grace offered by our Lord and Savior Jesus Christ. Faith in (allegiance to) Him clears the way for all the other loving things they get from us and connects them to the One directing our efforts. A bottle of water on a hot day gives relief for a moment. Grace gives relief for an eternity.

Middles are immediately uncertain when we explain that evangelism is for every disciple, not just the ones who have a gift for it. "I'm not qualified. I don't know enough Bible. I'm afraid I can't answer their questions. What if I say something wrong?"

This aggravated me as a teacher until I stopped misinterpreting it. I believed they were insecure or lazy or feigning ignorance, especially if the Middle was a long-time believer who'd been to church for a decade or more. All those Bible studies? All those sermons? All those years as a believer and they still don't know? Some Middles need to be challenged with those questions.

But most are exposing the weakness in our teaching, not the weakness in their character. We are failing them by our unwillingness to make the process of evangelism attainable for them. For many Middles, talking to someone about Jesus is for the pastor and the Type-A's at the top. This isn't a copout. It's what they've been taught by either example or exasperation.

I struggle with it, too. Why is it so hard to share my faith?

Because my concept of sharing my faith is the same as my concept of giving a sermon. Honestly, I think my job is to give a talk that convinces someone to believe in Jesus. If I do the talk right, Not Yets will say yes. If I do it wrong, Not Yets will remain Not Yets. So much pressure. So little reward.

I once heard Andy Stanley talk about clarifying the win. He said if we define a win on Sunday morning as someone committing to Jesus, we will have a lot of unsuccessful Sundays. Instead, he defines a win on Sunday morning as someone wanting to come back next week and bring a friend. Does this mean he doesn't care about people coming to know Jesus? No. He assumes if someone wants to be where the Gospel is presented, they will eventually believe. And if they bring a friend, chances are good the friend will eventually believe, too.

In the same way, we need a way to show Middles that an evangelistic win is not dictated by the success of a single talk that leads to a particular decision. A win is dictated by a better understanding of the grace that saves. If the average disciple lives life in grace, he will bless God by blessing others. When others are blessed, God prompts them to ask the questions that allow us to share the Way. Which set me thinking more deeply than ever before.

What does it mean to be a disciple-maker?

LIVING GRACE, BLESSING OTHERS, SHARING THE WAY

I am a Middle. I think God wants me to be a disciple(maker) of Jesus, but I'm confused by what the Church is teaching. This is what I'm hearing from the pulpit and the Bible studies and the small groups (from *my own teaching* at times!):

1. Jesus died for me and rose again to pay the penalty for my sins so I could spend eternity with Him. That's called grace.
2. If I believe in Him, that grace covers me. Now, when God looks at me, He sees the perfection of His Son.
3. Somehow, I receive the Holy Spirit to guide and direct me to live for God.
4. Now, I must clean up my act and obey all His laws as determined by my denomination. My pastor will help me with lessons on what those entail. My brothers and sisters will complement those lessons with social lessons and Bible studies so I can understand what I'm supposed to do.
5. If I do those things, God and the church will be pleased. If I don't do those things, God and the church will be upset.

In other words, once I receive grace for salvation, I must follow the laws of God and the church so I can be a better person. Which, if you think about it, is like taking a nice hot shower to get clean and then putting your smelly gym clothes back on. Sure, grace gets you clean, but you must wear the law to stay that way. It doesn't make sense. What you wear (what you do) didn't get you clean. How can it keep you clean? (Think of this analogy and read Colossians 3:1-17.)

Why do we think that way? Because we misunderstand the purpose of discipleship. We think becoming a disciple(maker) is knowing more so we can act better as people. If I believe in Jesus and study His Word, He will help me parent better, love my spouse better, keep my word better, clean up my cursing and my addictions and my bad habits. Bonus! He will also bless me with a better life, a better job, a better car, a better family, a better everything! We fail at discipling the Middle because we tell the Middle that disciple-making is about producing a better you for you.

And here's the crazy thing—purely anecdotal, but it's been true in each of the places I've ministered—the Middles are *already* pretty good people! They aren't causing disruptions in the church. They aren't fighting all the changes. They aren't always pew potatoes, sitting around waiting to see what's on the channel this Sunday. They aren't starting new ministries, either, let's be honest, but the greatest concern about them is to wake them up, not to clear up their sin or field their complaints. When they hear disciple-making is about being better for themselves, it sounds, well, unnecessary. It can even lead Middles to wonder if Christianity is for them.

A Middle knows she is sinful. A Middle knows he isn't a fired-up follower. A Middle knows she is missing the abundant life somehow. But if the abundant life is about making myself better, then I either see how much I fail at it or I don't know that I have enough sin to carve out of my life to reap that benefit.

In fact, a thoughtful Middle might even see the pursuit of a better self as what it is: selfish!

Is doing good deeds selfish? If we feel so good after doing something good for someone, are we doing it to get the feeling, or are we doing it for the person? A waking Middle probably came up with that question.

I remember asking myself that question. I also remember dropping to my knees one night as I sought God's direction. How do I teach disciple-making if it means teaching people to rely on grace for salvation but law for abundant life? Eventually, God helped me to see this dichotomy and led me to a different question.

When we put our faith in (give allegiance to) Jesus (and do whatever steps our denomination requires), we are covered by His blood, correct? When we accept the grace of God, our sins are completely forgiven, right? When we choose to follow the Way of Christ, God looks at us and sees perfection, right?

Then why aren't we suddenly bathed in angelic light? Why don't we (metaphorically) sprout wings and get a harp and ascend to heaven immediately? But we don't. God leaves us here on this earth. Why? To make us *more* perfect? How can something perfect be more perfect? God is taking a huge risk. Leaving us here guarantees we are going to mar that perfection. God is putting Himself on the hook for even more grace, isn't He?

The question I asked is, "Once we are saved, why doesn't He bring us instantly into heaven?"

Answer: the mission.

God didn't snatch me up to heaven when I believed because He has chosen to use me to reach more people. I might be a preacher, an accountant, a janitor, a President, a housewife, a disabled vet, or a homeless person. I might be healthy, young, old, sick, living or dying. Regardless of my status in this life, God leaves me here to reach one more. How has He chosen to do that through me? By sanctifying me. He wants people around me to see the transformation in me so they will ask how that change was wrought. My answer is Jesus. And He offers it to them, too.

In other words, my salvation is for me, but disciple-making is not for me. It's for them.

This concept will take more fleshing out later, but right now follow my line of thinking. To display grace and attract others to the faith, I need to learn to live in grace, not law. When I live in grace, I will be drawn to love God more, which in turn draws me to bless others and love them too much to avoid sharing The Way with them. Is this concept in Scripture, or am I just finding my own path?

I believe the Word not only validates this idea, but has a whole letter devoted to it.

> *For through the law, I died to the law, so that I might live to God. I have been crucified with Christ. It is no longer I who live, but Christ who lives in me. And the life I now*

live in the flesh, I live by faith in the Son of God, who loved me and gave Himself for me. I do not nullify the grace of God, for if righteousness were through the law, then Christ died for no purpose.

— Galatians 2:19-21

Let me ask you only this: Did you receive the Spirit by works of the law or by hearing with faith? Are you so foolish? Having begun by the Spirit, are you now being perfected by the flesh? . . . Does He Who supplies the Spirit do so by works of the law or by hearing with faith . . .

— Galatians 3:2-5

For you were called to freedom, brothers. Only do not use your freedom as an opportunity for the flesh, but through love serve one another. For the whole law is fulfilled in one word: 'You shall love your neighbor as yourself.'

— Galatians 5:13-14

Paul is entreating the Galatians not to let anyone fall back under the law when they can live in the Spirit under grace. Near the end of his impassioned letter, he writes the law is fulfilled in blessing others starting with the household of God (Galatians 6:10).

I am not advocating the dismissal of the Law—as Jesus said, "not an iota, not a dot, will pass from the Law until all is accomplished" (Matthew 5:18, ESV). I am saying we live in the Spirit by grace in such a way the Law is honored, and the people around us are influenced.

The best passage I've found to teach this concept is in 2 Peter 1:1-8. In them, God shows us what a disciple is, who disciples become, and the purpose of being a disciple (*hint: making disciples*). In the following chapters, we will lay a foundation and build our disciple-making one story at a time—what it is, who they become, and their mission. As we do, remember the third floor doesn't float—it requires the foundation and the first two floors to be what it is.

ARE YOU IN?

Maybe you're a Middle. Maybe you've wondered if church, if being a disciple(maker), if even the faith (allegiance) is for you. My hope is to convince you that being a disciple(maker) is so attainable and desirable that you will gladly sign up to live in grace, bless others, and share The Way. If you do, you will find out that faith (allegiance) was meant for you, and the church was meant to help you find it. Join the rest of us in the Middle Group as we explore together what it truly means to live in Christ.

If you're one of those Type-A's on reconnaissance to see what those crazy Middles are doing, I have one word for you: Welcome! We need Grace Agents who are go-getters and want to hand out this book to Middles and Others and even help teach them to be a disciple(maker). Who knows? You might learn something, too!

If you're one of the Others, the 10%, and someone handed you this book, don't put it down. You don't have to aim for the top—just aim for the Middle. We believe in you, and so does Jesus!

Are you in? Then, from one Middle to another, I'm praying God uses us to serve one more, reach one more, teach one more, and help one more grow in Christ.

PART 2

BE

BELIEVE:
Am I Engaged to God?

If we are going to rethink (repent of) our view of the church and give allegiance to (put our faith in) King Jesus, we can't use our "label" to excuse us from the mission to become His disciple(maker). Type-A's will struggle submitting to the King, and Others will struggle to keep their commitment. Middles will struggle to believe they can be used. Regardless of our struggle, our new perspective and our allegiance both prepare and require us to find out how to be on a mission.

Now that we KNOW disciple-making is for God and not us and that we are all called to it, we must learn to BE what God asks us to be—a disciple(maker)—so that we can LIVE out His purpose.

KNOW, BE, LIVE

In many ways, what we believe about a god determines what we believe about everything else. Don't be thrown off by the "little g" god in the following. I'm doing this out of respect for our thought process.

What if my god is indifferent, creating the world and then stepping back to let it wind down like a clock? I will give a nod to god but have no formal way of worshiping. Unless worship is important to me, that is, because all my decisions will be based on what I think is right or wrong. I will have respect for life but be unwilling to dictate to others how life should be honored.

If my god is a tyrant, creating mankind and then standing over them, waiting to catch them doing something wrong? I will worship to appease, seeking ritual so I know I'm "doing it right." All my decisions will be based on what god says is right or wrong, and I will judge others with the same measuring stick. I will have respect for life and dictate to the people around me how god wants life to be honored.

If I have no god, believing the world was formed by natural forces? I will worship the highest power I know—often myself but at times other people or organizations I deem superior. All my decisions will be based on what is socially accepted as right or wrong (unless I disagree). I may have respect for life, but often only as it affects me personally. I may not respect life at all—who says I must?

If my god is gracious, creating mankind to love them and grow them and redeem them? I will worship because god is good. My decisions will be based on what I believe god sees as right and wrong, but I will not expect those around me to act the same until they also believe. I will have respect for life and will try to instill that same respect in others.

This last, of course, is Jesus. He is not an indifferent creator, watching the world spin and letting us get by on our own. He is not a tyrant, waiting for us to sin so He can send us to hell. He is not a social construct I use to determine how I will live.

He is the God of grace, loving me, growing me, redeeming me for my own sake but also so He might redeem others. He is the God of truth, showing me, prodding me, and encouraging me to live in the best way He designed for me. I want to follow Him, make Him proud, and be like Him, but that doesn't mean I *have* to obey Him for Him to love me. He is gracious, and I am amazed. He is truth, and I am in awe.

In the same way, what we believe about being a disciple(maker) determines how we follow God (are you glad the capital G is back?).

For a long time, I believed in the gracious God but acted as if He was one of the other three. Yes, Jesus loves me, but He's too busy to notice my circumstances; it would be wrong even to bring my situation up to Him. Yes, Jesus loves me, so long as I adhere to the restrictions and rules; it would be wrong to think I'm ever going to measure up (and have you seen what that other guy is doing/not doing?). Yes, Jesus loves me, but I'm going to live my life however I want; His grace will cover it.

As my understanding has deepened, I've realized how I follow Jesus reveals my faith in (allegiance to) Jesus. I can know the right things and even live out many of the right things without becoming what Jesus has in mind for me. Often in the church, we unwittingly teach what every other religion teaches:

1. Know about God and what God expects.
2. Do what God expects.
3. Reap the consequences or rewards.

Isn't it obvious? This is living by law. The Father spent most of the history of mankind proving to us we can't accomplish this (we call it the Old Testament). Under the new covenant, Jesus taught we must have an even greater righteousness than this (Matthew 5:20). How is that possible? Grace. How does grace change our teaching?

In the Sermon on the Mount (Matthew, chapters 5-7), Jesus spends 20 verses helping us understand what God expects, 62 verses explaining who we are to be, and the final 27 verses telling us how to live it out (the final two verses are a reaction from the crowd). Each section contains hints of the other two, but they can be distilled into these three steps:

1. Know about God and what God expects.
2. Be who God calls you to be.
3. Live out who you are now.

As Jesus explains about God and what He expects, He also tells us who to be and how to live it out. As Jesus explains who God calls us to be, He also helps us know God and live out who we are in Him. As Jesus explains how to live out who we are now, He also helps us know God and be who He calls us to be. The three are intertwined, but the "Be" is where grace lives.

Be a disciple(maker) of Jesus.

Today, we understand what His first audience did not: God's plan is perfected in the death and resurrection of the Son of God. Suddenly, we can no longer define God in three steps.

1. Know about God and what God expects.
2. Be who God calls you to be.
3. Recognize that you fall short.
4. Fall on the grace of Jesus for forgiveness and new life.
5. Be who God saved you to be.
6. Live out who you are now to influence others.

But in the teaching of Jesus, even before His sacrifice, we see grace is the heart of the truth of God. To be a disciple(maker) is to live in grace.

What does that mean?

GOOD NEWS

This is where most disciple-making books start to lose me. With a heartfelt story about how the author was going about it all wrong, I am told that a better, deeper, richer life is available if only . . .

    . . . I would have a ministry experience in a position I don't hold.
    . . . I would have a missions experience on a trip I can't afford.
    . . . I would have a tragic experience I can't manufacture.
    . . . I would really, really, really commit to obedience to the Lord.

I don't get lost because I don't agree with what they are saying. I get it and even admire it. I don't get lost because I can't understand what they're saying. I love hearing stories that move people of faith to greater faith, so I'm not put off by the content. My issue isn't that I can't relate to what I'm being told. I don't begrudge these great men and women of God their testimonies—actually, I admire them, envy them.

It's just that I can't follow.

So here is some great news. The Good News is all you need to become a disciple(maker). Your story, whatever it is, and your decision to follow Jesus is enough. Where you are and who you are right now is enough to get started. Made new by grace, you are also prompted by grace to live in grace. But how do you do that?

Don't let yourself skip this part. It's basic, I know, but the beauty of the base is that it holds up everything else. Don't think of what I'm about to say as a few paragraphs to skip over. Think of it as preparing to be a disciple(maker). Important. True. Foundational.

God created the world and gave it to mankind. Because of their relationship, mankind needed no set of rules. God walked with them in the cool of the day. But God offered them free will by giving them a choice. Mankind decided to eat of the tree of the knowledge of good and evil. When they did, they broke their relationship with God. We proved our lack of integrity. We proved our pride. We proved our desire to be god of our world.

God calls that sin.

Sin crouched at man's door, invading at every opportunity. The enemy, Satan, whispered in our ears, and we listened and went our own way. Murder followed. Thieving. Lying—the parasite sin, feeding off other sins and compounding errors—soon followed. We convince ourselves we are generally good people, but we can't even follow the rules we set for ourselves. We break relationships, we cut corners, we tell half-truths and white lies.

God is not surprised. He knew from the beginning this would happen. To prove to us we can't do it on our own, He let us try. Tribal nomads. Clans and ethnic groups. Fledgling nations. He gave us laws as a fence and asked us to behave, to stay in the yard, to be good children for Him. We wanted to rule ourselves. Judges, monarchies, and dictatorships. Republics and democracies. Socialism, Communism, Progressivism, Liberalism, Conservatism, Capitalism. Every way we tried to govern ourselves, our selfishness and unfairness, our pride and arrogance, has caused us to fail each other in numerous ways.

In the middle of it all, God shaped a people for the sake of identification. They were not inherently special, except that God chose to work through them to show the world it needed saving and then to save it. They were protected when they were obedient and rejected when they rebelled. Faithful people kept coming back to God. He blessed them by keeping a straight line from their father, Abraham, to the coming Messiah, who would change the world. When the world was ripe for change—civilization connected by Roman roads, commerce and education connected by Greek language, religion in tumult from worshiping people to worshiping idols to worshiping caricatures of God—He sent His Son.

The world did not know Him, but He knew His mission. He came to tell us the Kingdom of Heaven is at hand. I imagine Him standing before a crowd of people, holding out His hands, pleading as He says this. Little did the people know the Kingdom of Heaven was at *His hands*. The ones that touched and healed. The ones that waved as He taught. The ones that opened the scrolls of Scripture. The ones pierced by nails.

Jesus, friend of sinners, allowed Himself to be arrested without charge, prosecuted unlawfully, convicted without guilt, beaten without cause, and crucified without protest. His great physical pain—the beatings, the crown of thorns, the nail-pierced hands and feet—only exceeded by the spiritual, mental, and emotional pain of His ordeal. Separated from His Father, all the sin of all the world for all time crashed down on

Him, and He *became* sin—what does that do to a person? How did He survive it?

He was pierced, bled out, and buried in another's tomb. Jesus, Son of God, was dead.

But Sunday came, and just as the women wondered how to roll back the stone to give the body of their dear leader the treatment it deserved, they are surprised by angels. Jesus is risen! He is risen, indeed! (Notice they say He is risen, not He was raised.) They couldn't believe it, and neither could the apostles, but Jesus proved over and over to hundreds of people that He defeated death and offered eternal redemption for all those who believe.

If you rethink (repent of) your life so far and put faith in (give allegiance to) this Jesus, He offers you forgiveness, the Spirit, and eternal life.

You. Are. Saved. Your sins are no longer counted against you. Your relationship with God has been restored. The covenant of the Father has been kept. Your faith has made you well.

Good News, right?

NOW WHAT?

Would it surprise you if I said God was not in the business of saving souls? Yes, I know that's important to Him. I'm glad it is! But as I read through the Scripture, I see a larger plan than just saving us. He wants more than to give you a "Get out of jail free!" card. He wants more than to give you citizenship in Heaven.

God is in the business of redemption.

Creation knows it. In the letter to the Romans, Paul gives us some insight into how creation feels about waiting around for us to get it.

> *For the creation was subjected to futility, not willingly, but because of Him Who subjected it, in hope that the creation itself will be set free from its bondage to corruption and obtain the freedom of the glory of the children of God. For we know that the whole creation has been groaning together in the pains of childbirth until now.*
>
> *— Romans 8:20-22*

Creation is waiting on the culmination of God's human project to be everything God intended it to be. Creation is waiting to be redeemed.

Mankind is too often satisfied with salvation. We explore this God who says He loves us despite our sins, discover His Son and what He did to free us, and accept His offer of release from guilt and shame. We are convicted, condemned, convinced, and made alive in the Spirit by the Good News of Jesus Christ. And then what?

Most denominations ask people to make a confession of faith. Generally, we have them say something like, "I believe that Jesus is the Christ, the Son of the Living God, and He is my Lord and Savior." Savior, yes. And Lord. Because of His love for us, we owe no debt to Him for His sacrifice, not even a debt of gratitude. When we accept His offer of salvation, though, we also ask Him to be Lord of our lives. We believe His work in us is just starting. He wants to redeem us—buy us back and make us the valuable person He always intended us to be. How can we honor God's desire?

By becoming a disciple(maker) for His Son. We don't *have to* follow Jesus. We *get to* follow Jesus. We don't *have to* obey His rules. We *get to* learn how to live, love, laugh, and cry like Jesus. No one is going to walk on water or feed five thousand with a few loaves and fish (although He can choose to heal through us and any number of other miraculous things). Jesus isn't calling us to miracles, He's calling us to holiness. Miracles attest to holiness, but holiness is the goal of redemption. One day we will get to Heaven; right now, God wants the world to see us strive toward holiness. What is holiness? Being set apart for Him.

You and I get to be a disciple(maker).

But what is it?

THINK, SPEAK, ACT, LOOK, SMELL

A story in the book of John gives us a hint. Chapter Nine tells the story of a man blind since birth. The disciples of Jesus, eager to prove to their teacher how much they understand God, ask Jesus if the man is blind because he has sinned or because his parents sinned. Jesus proves how little they know about God by responding,

It was not that this man sinned, or his parents, but that the works of God might be displayed in him. We must work the works of Him who sent Me while it is day; night is coming, when no one can work. As long as I am in the world, I am the light of the world.

— *John 9:3-5*

Jesus rebukes the notion that the man's misfortune is from sin. Instead, He says God is using the misfortune of the man in a mighty way. Then He heals the man. We get three lessons from His response:

1. Unfortunate circumstances are not always caused by sin. Life happens.
2. Unfortunate circumstances are opportunities for God to show His power and love.
3. A disciple(maker) of Jesus looks for God's opportunities.
4. Miracles follow our willingness to meet God's opportunities.

    Part of being a disciple(maker), then, is looking for God's opportunities. We'll discuss that more later. For now, let's return to the story.

    The neighbors are amazed to see this man they know has always been blind. They just couldn't believe it, but the man confirmed who he was. His detractors wanted to know how it was possible, so he told them the story. Immediately, those same people wanted to know where to find Jesus. We learn a fifth lesson about being a disciple here, don't we? The man knows only that Jesus healed him, but that is enough to point the neighbors to his Healer. They immediately want to know where He is.

5. To respond to God's opportunities is to use the knowledge of Him we have.

In stark contrast, the Pharisees question everything, but none of them want to know Jesus. Instead, they want to investigate if it happened, what really happened, how it was really done, and who really did it. They want to talk to the parents to see if the man is lying. The parents are so scared of being connected to Jesus that they throw their own son under the bus even as they confirm his blindness. The religious leaders of the day bring the man back to them.

So for the second time they called the man who had been blind and said to him, "Give glory to God. We know that this man is a sinner."

He answered, "Whether he is a sinner I do not know. One thing I do know, that though I was blind, now I see."

They said to him, "What did He do to you? How did He open your eyes?"

— *John 9:24-26*

This is important. Don't miss this. All the Pharisees are doing is cross-examining. They have already heard the story. They know all the answers, but they are trying to catch the man in a lie. As they start asking questions, though, the man seems to get fed up. He's heard enough, so he replies to their questions with a note of sarcasm:

> *He answered them, "I have told you already, and you would not listen. Why do you want to hear it again? Do you also want to become His disciples?"*
>
> *— John 9:27*

Catch that? Of course, he's being salty. He's catching their discomfort and needling them with their greatest fear—to be identified with Jesus. But don't miss this lesson about being a disciple(maker). Why did he say this? And why did the Pharisees immediately respond by claiming to be disciples of Moses? Because the barb was understood through the lens of what a disciple(maker) is.

We start there.

A disciple(maker) is not someone who hears about a teacher and becomes a fan. A disciple(maker) is not someone who listens to a teacher and takes to heart the lessons that make sense to him. A disciple(maker) is not someone who spends a semester with a teacher and gets comfortable with a body of knowledge.

A disciple(maker) is someone who studies to think like the rabbi, look like him, act like him, speak like him, and *smell* like him. A disciple spends every day in the company of the rabbi, trying to drink in all the rabbi is. A disciple wants to know how the rabbi interacts with people and how he acts when he is alone. He wants to know when the rabbi prays and how. He wants to know what the rabbi's teaching looks like when it is lived out. He wants to be as much like the rabbi as he possibly can.

> *"A disciple is not above his teacher, nor a servant above his master. It is enough for the disciple to be like his teacher, and the servant like his master."*
>
> — *Matthew 10:24-25a*

It isn't enough to hear the Rabbi's teaching and do some of the things he says. The true disciple(maker) won't settle for that.

He will want to become what the Rabbi is so that he can also learn to make disciples.

This is why so many discipleship books talk about the experience/tragedy/circumstance that led them to a deep level of faith. Something made them recognize following Jesus is much more serious than going to church, hearing a few sermons, and becoming a better person. It's a lifestyle, a commitment, a decision to be changed.

Don't be scared, and don't wall up. I'm just getting started. Remember the Good News? Don't let go of the Gospel. You are saved by grace, people, not by smelling like Jesus. Before you shelve this book, make it to the end of the next section. I promise there's hope for the Middle in you that is balking at such a high calling...

GOOD NEWS, GREAT COMMISSION

No surprise that being a disciple(maker) means commitment, right?

I think Middles have two reasons they are afraid to commit. Some of us are just not very good at commitment. We start out well, maybe, but fizzle out. Diets, exercise programs, book clubs, church, anything that asks for a daily or weekly schedule taxes this Middle's ability to stay focused.

The other Middles are too good at commitment. We know that when we start something, it means all in or nothing at all. The idea of starting a new way of life is daunting. How do we know it will work, and what if it doesn't? This Middle's anxiety keeps them unfocused.

I have Good News for both kinds. Jesus saved you by grace and plans to mold you by grace, as well. For those who struggle with commitment, know God sees you the way I saw my children learning to walk. After holding on to something and pulling themselves up, eventually my kids got brave and turned to see me. With my encouragement, each one let go and started my way. Every one of them got a step or two into their first foray and fell on their diaper.

Can you imagine what others would say if I had straightened up and said, "I can't believe you! What kind of effort is that? If you act like you're going to walk to me, you better make it all the way!" Instead, what does a good parent do? We make light of the fall, get them back on their feet, tell them what a great job they did, and encourage them to try again.

God does the same with us. That's grace. Because of our perfection in His Son, He's not about single attempts. He's all about teaching us to walk. As we learn to walk, He's not about our pace. He's about teaching us to run. As we learn to run, He's not worried about our endurance. He's about teaching us to rest.

No two of my four kids walked at the same age. One of them eventually ran cross country, one played football, one preferred academic pursuits, and one fell in love with artistic performance (all different forms of running). I don't judge them based on how they run. I love them for how they run. God is the same with us. He wants what is best for us, but grace allows us to go at the pace we can.

For those who know once they commit they won't turn back, God sees your loyalty and can't wait to meet you with His own. When my kids trust me for something, I delight in proving trustworthy. I want them to know they can count on me because if I let them down, they may not trust me again. Because I am human, sometimes I fail. Maybe someone has failed you, too, and now you don't know if you can trust anyone. Even God.

Good News! Grace covers that, too. God loves you so much He was willing to die for you. Do you think a little doubt will keep Him away? The Bible histories, psalms, and sayings are full of people doubting God but finding out God keeps His promises. Does their doubt in His goodness change His goodness?

The saying is trustworthy, for if we have died with Him, we will also live with Him; if we endure, we will also reign with Him; if we deny Him, He will also deny us; if we are faithless, He remains faithful—for He cannot disown Himself.

— *2 Timothy 2:11-13*

God is trustworthy. He rescued us and gave us a position of royalty and all we need do is acknowledge Him. If, at times, we do not live up to our faith, He remains faithful. He is so loyal, He out-loyals us. When you commit to Him, even if your commitment wavers, His will not.

That's Good News!

Maybe you still want to be cautious. What exactly is your commitment? I believe that's answered by that awesome passage in Matthew where Jesus gives His last word before ascending to heaven. We're going to start a few verses before.

Now the eleven disciples went to Galilee, to the mountain to which Jesus had directed them. And when they saw Him they worshiped Him, but some doubted.

— *Matthew 28:16-17*

Exciting revelation for those afraid to commit: some disciples still doubted *even as they watched Jesus ascend to heaven!* How is that possible? I'd like to think if I saw Jesus rise from the dead, appear and disappear at will, teach me forty days about my part in the Kingdom, and then somehow float up into Heaven, I'd have no doubts left. Not so for the disciples. Remember that Paul says Jesus appeared to 500 (1 Corinthians 15:6), but only 120 gathered in the room to receive the Holy Spirit (Acts 1:15).

Not so for us, either. What did they doubt? The text doesn't tell us. All we know for certain is that doubt existed. I'm wondering about it, though. Maybe they doubted what He told them. Maybe they had a hard time wrapping their minds around the reality of what they had experienced. Maybe they doubted He was God and not some apparition leading them astray. In other words, maybe they had all the same doubts we have today.

Doubt is common in matters of faith, and God is not afraid of it. He's able to answer all your doubts, even if you are not. Our saying at The Jar is, "Doubts are just questions that haven't been answered yet." When you confess Jesus as Savior *and* Lord, remember that doubt will not leave completely. In fact, God will often use it to deepen your faith. Notice what Jesus says next to those who worshiped and to those who doubted.

> *And Jesus came and said to them, "All authority in heaven and on earth has been given to me. As you go therefore, make disciples of all nations, baptizing them in the name of the Father and of the Son and of the Holy Spirit, teaching them to observe all that I have commanded you. And behold, I am with you always, to the end of the age.*
> *— Matthew 28:18-20 (emphasis on my changes)*

As we go into our world, wherever we are planted, wherever we are led, wherever we work or play or learn or teach or laugh or cry, we are to help people receive the grace of Christ and learn to look like Him, think like Him, speak like Him, act like Him, smell like Him if we can. God makes the most of our environment, our upbringing, our morality, our past mistakes, our character, and reputation, who we were when we committed to Him, and asks us to use all those things that make us who we are to serve one more, reach one more, teach one more, help one more grow in Christ.

I don't do anything special to be a disciple(maker). I just take Jesus with me wherever I go.

Won't days come when we question that? This passage implicitly guarantees that. Despite any experiences we've had with Jesus, none of us saw Him after His resurrection. If those who did doubted, how can we expect ourselves to live without doubt? The question isn't if we will doubt, but what will keep us faithful in our allegiance when we do.

How about a little Christmas?

When Mary becomes pregnant with Jesus, she and Joseph are betrothed. Well, engaged; but if I say engaged, you may struggle with this concept. In our modern world, getting engaged is often really an announcement of an impending wedding. Sometimes, it's just a chance to put off the wedding, but we feel like we are one step closer. During the first century, however, Jewish custom considered the commitment to get engaged as binding as the marriage—like the betrothal in the Middle Ages. The engagement signified a contract between two families to meld into one. Breaking it meant a breach of covenant. This is why Joseph's decision to keep his pledge to Mary is so important to the Christmas story.

Paul often talks about the Holy Spirit being a pledge, a guarantee, of our salvation. Our faith (allegiance) to Jesus is like a betrothal to Him, an engagement that signifies a covenant. The marriage, if you will, is our entrance into heaven, but that doesn't diminish the engagement. In fact, marriage would be impossible without it. Because we gave our hearts to Jesus that day and because God is faithful, we can rest in blessed assurance that the wedding will occur, and we will be forever united with Christ.

God knew we would need a reminder of that commitment. An engagement ring, so to speak. Something we can look back on when we question the validity of that decision. Imagine you are a believer, and you've been going through a tough time. Losing your way, you have lived without acknowledging God for a while and are just now realizing it. You want to come back. Can you? How do you know God will take you back? How do you know He will honor His commitment even if you've strayed?

What shall we say then? Are we to continue in sin that grace may abound? By no means! How can we who died to sin still live in it? Do you not know that all of us who have been baptized into Christ Jesus were baptized into His death? We were buried therefore with Him by baptism into death, in order that, just as Christ was raised from the dead by the glory of the Father, we too might walk in newness of life.

— Romans 6:1-4, ESV

Baptism is a controversial topic in the church. Some believe it is a part of salvation. Some believe it is the first step after salvation. Some believe there is a separate baptism of the Holy Spirit. Some believe in infant baptism. Some believe in sprinkling. Please don't get caught up here in our differences. Remember our fences? We are focusing on what we have in common.

Regardless of your personal belief about baptism, this passage has one thing in common for us all. Baptism allows us to look back and see the commitment we've made. It's a day we can point to and say, "See? I'm engaged! I was (already) saved that day! I was sprinkled/immersed and received (the baptism of) the Holy Spirit that day! I am His! It reminds me that my old self is dead and the person I am today is different. I am betrothed to my God, and He will not let me go!"

Disciple-making is wanting to think like Jesus, speak like Jesus, look like Jesus, act like Jesus, and smell like Jesus because of the Good News of His grace. Baptism is the reminder that He has accepted me despite who I am and will not give up on me. When I have bad days, I look to that glorious day and thank Jesus for His grace. It reminds me of my commitment, and I'm encouraged to be faithful to the One who is faithful to me.

In Him [Christ] you also, when you heard the word of truth, the gospel of your salvation, and believed in Him,

were sealed with the promised Holy Spirit, who is the guarantee of our inheritance until we acquire possession of it, to the praise of His glory.
        — Ephesians 1:13-14 [brackets mine]

Armed with my betrothal to the God who saved me and my desire to smell like His Son, all I need now is an understanding of my part in the mission: to show others The Way and lead them to a similar engagement with God.

JESUS WITH SKIN

As we go, wherever we go, we show Jesus in us so people might follow Jesus as well, remembering we were sealed with His Spirit. As we cling to the finished work of Christ, what does it mean to do the unfinished work of His disciple(maker)s?

. . . baptizing them in the name of the Father and of the Son and of the Holy Spirit, teaching them to observe all that I have commanded you.
        — Matthew 28:19b-20a, ESV

I know, Middles. I'm afraid of talking about the Trinity, too. Let me just say this. I take comfort in how difficult it is to explain the Trinity. I am encouraged that no amount of study and research gets me much closer to understanding it. Know why? Because if God is greater than us, it stands to reason that He will be beyond explanation. Inexplicable.

Theologians go on and on about how God is all-knowing (omniscient), all-powerful (omnipotent), ever-present (omnipresent), and never-changing (immutable). Those are all great characteristics necessary in a god to prove divinity. Nearly every religion has some sense of this, even if they use a thousand gods to cover these attributes completely. What makes my faith in God sing is my inability to describe what it means that God is three in one, one in three.

I have no problem with the divinity of the Father, but the personal Father depicted in the Bible gives me peace that He is intimately involved with my life.

I have no problem with the personal Jesus, but His divinity gives me hope that He is intimately able to treat my sin once and for all.

I have no idea what it means for the Spirit to be divine or personal, but He is like the wind—I can see where He is by the work He does, but I must watch to see where He's been or where He's going.

God is bigger than I can imagine. When Jesus tells us to baptize in the name of the Father, the Son, and the Holy Spirit, I bask in the brilliance of an inexplicable God and wonder what I might learn about Him next. It's a little scarier, actually, to consider teaching other people all that Jesus commanded.

I've been told the Jews had over 600 laws. Christ came along and said He wasn't changing an iota of the law but fulfilling it. I've been taught Jesus added intent, motivation, and heart to those laws to make them even more demanding.

I know God gave me these laws as fences to help me stay in the yard, but sometimes I feel like the laws also create an obstacle course in the yard. Sometimes, I'm crawling under barbed wire; sometimes, I'm scaling an unattainable wall. The slalom through hoops of fire? Hate that part. How can I make sense enough of all the guidelines for myself? If I can't do that, how can I teach all that is commanded?

If I focus on the Law, I can't. But if I focus on the heart of the law, I find grace.

> *But when the Pharisees heard that He had silenced the Sadducees, they gathered together. And one of them, a lawyer, asked Him a question to test Him. "Teacher, which is the great commandment in the Law?"*
>
> *And He said to him, "You shall love the Lord your God with all your heart and with all your soul and with all your mind. This is the first and great commandment. And a second is like it: You shall love your neighbor as yourself. On these two commandments depend all the Law and the Prophets.*
>
> *— Matthew 22:34-40*

When we find grace, we learn to love God and ourselves this way. When we live in grace, we find the grace to love ourselves and people this way. Which, by the way, leads us to love God even more.

91

That's why my wife calls the Mosaic Law God's "Love Laws." Even those crazy sacrificial laws were given out of love to help followers atone for their sin and renew their relationship with God. Jesus has replaced those particular laws with Himself, the greatest fulfillment of Love Laws ever.

How can we learn to follow all the other Love Laws?

Live in grace, bless others, and share The Way. Here is where disciple(maker)s live because it's where our Rabbi lives. Here is where our Rabbi lives because it's where His Father lives. Here is where the Spirit lives because He lives to reveal the Father and the Son. Living in grace doesn't mean living how we feel like living. Instead, it means being an example of grace to every person we meet so they will see the Living God in us and crave what God can do for them. I call it Gospel living.

Jesus isn't asking all of us to be high school teachers or college professors, Sunday school leaders or small group facilitators, priests, or preachers. He's asking us to be Him to them. Jesus with skin.

IT'S ALL TOO MUCH

At this point, I wouldn't be upset if you thought I'd pulled a bait and switch. I tell you I understand Middles, tell you I know a way to be a disciple(maker) that Middles can do, and then I come back to much the same message as those other discipleship books. What gives?

Disciple-making isn't easier for Middles than it is for Type-A's if that's what you thought. I'm just being honest here. In fact (don't tell the Type-A's), this kind of disciple-making might be more difficult than what they are attempting. Being a disciple(maker) of Jesus, even with the reminder of baptism, carries with it the charge to deny ourselves and carry our cross. This is not different for us just because we see the world differently. Disciple-making, as God assigns it through the Good News, the Great Commission, and the Great Commandments, is difficult beyond words.

Jesus talks about the narrow way to righteousness. He tells us it's easier to get a camel through the eye of a needle than for a rich man to enter heaven. He tells us that our brothers and sisters may not believe God even after He sent Moses and the prophets and His only Son.

Have I given you false hope? Nope. I just haven't given you the whole lesson yet. We've skipped parts of the Great Commission that round it out. It's the first and last thing Jesus says that makes all the difference.

"All authority in heaven and on earth has been given to Me . . . and behold, I am with you always, to the end of the age."

— *Matthew 28:18b, 20b, ESV*

We shouldn't be surprised if thinking, looking, speaking, acting, and smelling like Jesus is too hard for us. He's God, after all. So, how can we approach disciple-making with any expectation of success? First, we remember the mission is not for us. It's for Him and for them. Then we remember that the One who has all the authority in existence has promised to be with us always to the end of the age. It's all too much unless Jesus is in the middle of it.

We're ready now to go to our main text and start seeing how to break the stronghold killing the Church. Peter gives us a detailed explanation about being a disciple(maker) at the beginning of his second letter. We're going to start here:

> *His divine power has granted to us all things that pertain to life and godliness . . .*
>
> — *2 Peter 1:3a*

To understand the importance of this verse, we must get to know a few words in Greek.

Divine power. Godly power. The Greek word for power is *dynamis* (pronounced doo-nam-is), from which we get the word "dynamite." The Godly dynamite of Jesus has granted to us, bestowed upon us, given to us all things. Not some things, not most things, not a few things. All things. What kinds of things? The ones that pertain to life and godliness.

Life. *Zoe* (zo-ay) encompasses all our lives—our mental, emotional, physical, spiritual, and social makeup.

God's powerful dynamite in Jesus has given us all things pertaining to our whole lives. And . . .

Godliness. *Eusebeio* (yoo-say-bay-o) means giving all to God, to worship Him with who we are. As we learned earlier, to naturally express our devotion to Him.

What does this mean? Not only has God, in His grace, saved us from our sin; He has given us every tool we need to live our lives completely sold out to Him. We already have it because of His dynamite power. We don't do it ourselves. He does it.

He uses our environment. How we grew up, what kind of family raised us, where we went to school. Our neighborhood, our residence, our workplace, our hangouts, even where we shop.

He uses our experience. The highs *and* the lows. The good and the bad. The healthy and the unhealthy. He gives us hope with the former and redemption for the latter.

He uses our personality. Introverts as well as extroverts. Thinking people and emotive people. Perceptive people and naïve people.

He uses our talents and gifts. Cooks and accountants. Actors and politicians. Tellers and storytellers. Wal-Mart employees and Target employees. Small business owners and hedge fund operators.

He uses our education. High school dropouts and doctorates. Certified welders and over-the-road truck drivers. Street smart and book smart.

He uses you and me. Where we are. With His power.

I thought you should know.

It's up to you to believe it.

BECOME:
A Grace Agent

Imagine a small group of people, a few more than ten, living in a community bereft of hope. Sure, religious institutions are trying to get people to behave. Political systems have been developed to punish people who don't behave. People have social gatherings that cross the social and economic spectrums—from the rich to the poor, from culture to ethnicity, from old to young, everyone has something they can do.

The community has everything it needs. Except hope.

Imagine this small group of people, maybe a dozen, learn something life-changing. They are awakened to a faith that offers salvation based on God's work, not theirs. They are called to create life change in the people around them. They are given supernatural power to accomplish the mission: bring hope to their community.

Twelve people, committed to a mission, drawing on a power greater than their own.

I'm not talking about the apostles in Jerusalem in the first century as recorded in the second chapter of Acts. I'm talking about you and the other followers of Jesus you know in your community today. What if God is calling you to be a Grace Agent for His Kingdom?

Scary, right?

All this is from God, who through Christ reconciled us to Himself and gave us the ministry of reconciliation; that is, in Christ, God was reconciling the world to Himself, not counting their trespasses against them, and entrusting to us the message of reconciliation.

— *2 Corinthians 5:18-19*

This is the second place where other discipleship books lose me. If I was able to get past the amazing discovery the author had in the first chapter, I get to the second chapter and find out God is looking for people to make a difference. I'm not sure I'm up to making a difference. I'm definitely not up to being Peter or Paul. I don't know how they did all they did, but I know it took all they had and then some. They were both martyred for it, but what bothers me as much or more is the way they sacrificed their lives *before* they were killed.

As my youngest son used to say, "Ain't nobody got time for that!"

I don't. Peter and the boys spent ten days locked in a room waiting for the Holy Spirit. Of course they did. They were homeless and jobless. I have both. I can't disappear for ten days waiting for something like that to happen. When the Holy Spirit did come, the whole tongues of fire and speaking in tongues happened. Regardless of our doctrine about Pentecost happening today, few of us—I'm going out on a limb and saying none of us—have experienced what they did. So, what are my credentials? What is my calling?

I'm just one guy. In my family, in my church, in my employment, in my community, what kind of effect can one guy have?

We just learned that being a disciple(maker) means thinking like Jesus, speaking like Jesus, acting like Jesus, and smelling like Jesus if we can. We are to be Jesus to the world, and Jesus is the hope of the world. We are the hope of the world. What kind of influence did Jesus have on His family? His disciples? His community? His nation? The world?

Sometimes, when we hear about the apostles and the great acts done by them as written in the Bible, we forget that none of them did anything. God did it all. Look at their efforts. All falls apart if God doesn't show up. If He doesn't give His power, they all start looking pretty foolish. No one gets healed. No one gets saved. No one gets included in the community of grace. If God isn't a part of what's happening in those stories, the stories aren't any more interesting than a personal diary.

Jesus changes all that, but He starts with the change in us. His divine power (godly dynamite) has granted to us (bestowed upon us, given to us) all things (not some things, not most things, not a few things) pertaining to life (mental, emotional, physical, social, spiritual) and godliness (devoting all our components of life to Him).

We don't have to lead a revolution. We *become* a revolution. We don't have to save the world ourselves. We become Grace Agents for the revolution that saves the world. We don't have to hold ten-day meetings waiting for the Holy Spirit. We become temples of the Holy Spirit. The hope given to us emanates from us in a way that brings hope to others.

Now, suppose one person in your family, church, employment, or community becomes a Grace Agent. Suppose the first thing that person does is seek out other Grace Agents. Suppose those two continue living the life they are already living, but they join in prayer and seek out another Grace Agent as they emanate hope to those around them.

This is what God intended when He created the church.

LET'S NOT GET AHEAD OF OURSELVES.

All God is asking of you is to be a disciple(maker) of Jesus, find other disciple(maker)s of Jesus, and bring hope to others so they will choose to be disciple(maker)s of Jesus. We do that by living in grace, blessing others, and sharing The Way. This is the mission of the church.

The mission is not to create a great Sunday morning service, encourage higher participation in Sunday School or small groups, meet our budgetary requirements, or create fun events for the youth or the family. The mission is to be the Church bringing hope through the Good News. All that other stuff is just our current toolbox.

I feel a bit overwhelmed when I think of being a disciple(maker) as starting (or even being a part of) a movement of people bringing significant change to my area of influence. I wish I didn't. God has given me certain skills. I'm a leader and a good manager of people. I'm a decent speaker. I'm a decent writer. I have a head for numbers so long as we don't bring in any algebraic equations. I love being around children, but in large numbers, they frighten me (can I get an amen?). God called me to use these skills as a lead pastor in a church.

Every day, I feel unworthy of the calling.

I know God is using me to reach others, but I often feel He does that despite my efforts. I know God is constantly moving me toward the likeness of His Son, but many days, I'm taking one step forward and two steps back (No, I didn't get that backward). I'd like to be the guy that starts a movement, but it's all I've got to move myself.

When God asked me to be a Grace Agent, I started looking for the exits. I knew movement in myself required enough power outside of me to make it possible. Until I could trust that power, I couldn't move beyond myself to affect others. I've lived with the idea of the Holy Spirit for a long time, but not until the last few years have I begun to understand the power available to us through Him.

Pentecostals are going, "All right!" Other denominations are going, "Oh no!"

I'm going to disappoint you both. This isn't a lead into spiritual gifts, but this is an acknowledgment that the Spirit is more than an also-ran in the Trinity. If we are truly interested in becoming disciple(maker)s of Jesus, we need to consider His promise.

> *But when the Helper comes, whom I will send to you from the Father, the Spirit of truth, who proceeds from the Father, He will bear witness about Me.*
>
> *— John 15:26*

> *I still have many things to say to you, but you cannot bear them now. When the Spirit of truth comes, He will guide you into all the truth, for He will not speak on His own authority, but whatever He hears He will speak, and He will declare to you the things that are to come. He will glorify me, for He will take what is Mine and declare it to you.*
>
> *— John 16:12-14*

When we hear that His divine power has been granted to us, we need to know what that power is. The Holy Spirit embodies that power and then resides in us and works through us to convict the world concerning sin and righteousness and judgment (John 16:8). But let's not get ahead of ourselves. First, we must know if we can trust the One giving us that power.

REPUTATION AND CHARACTER

When we meet a new person, we start with a clean slate. Whatever we've done in our past is unknown to the new person. They don't know our penchant to be a hothead, to cheat on our taxes, to lie to make stories better. They don't know we're loyal to a fault, love crocheting and basketball, and watch reruns of Friends incessantly. We get to remake ourselves.

But we don't. After a while, we are just who we are. If we aren't found out by our reputation, we are revealed by our character. People begin to think they know us well when they've been exposed to what we've done and how we operate. In other words, by our reputation and character.

His divine power has granted to us all things that pertain to life and godliness, through the knowledge of Him who called us to His own glory and excellence . . .
— 2 Peter 1:3 (emphasis mine)

- **Glory** – *doxa*, a person's renown, fame, reputation, and what others think of him.
- **Excellence** – *arete*, moral excellence, character, goodness beyond measure.

This is important. Peter tells us that the power granted to us for living a life of grace is through the knowledge of Jesus, who called us to His reputation and His goodness beyond measure. The Power comes from a Person who has perfect character—a sinless life, an unconditional love for all, an indomitable spirit. Jesus thought it all, said it all and did it all in absolute obedience to God for the glory of the Father. No character is greater.

How do we know? Because we have witnesses to all He has done. The historical accounts of Jesus' life written by Matthew, Mark, Luke, and John are called the Gospels. Gospel is another way of saying Good News. Good news is what those accounts are.

He was born of a virgin through a miraculous intervention of the Holy Spirit.

He was recognized as a baby by prophets to be the Messiah.

He was asking and teaching in the Temple at twelve and grew in wisdom and stature.

He was glorified by God and recognized by the second coming of Elijah at His baptism.

He was forty days in the desert, intimately tempted by Satan.

He healed people, loved people, taught people, admonished people, forgave people.

He was arrested, beaten, mocked, betrayed, killed, buried—and risen.

If I'm going to trust in the power of someone, I need to know them. I don't just want to take their word for it—I'm too cynical for that. But when everyone who knows him paints the same picture, I'm willing to put my cynicism aside and give the person a chance. Okay, Jesus. You get Your chance. I'm willing to get to know You. Before we go much further, though, what's in it for me?

Does that sound callous? Irreverent? Maybe it is, but when I was exploring Jesus, that was my question. Too often, I still go to Jesus, wondering what's in it for me. You may think Jesus minds, but I think He anticipated this in us. That's why we have so many of His promises.

Come to Him, and He will give you rest, Matthew 11:28-30.

Come to Him, and you walk in light instead of darkness, John 8:12.

Come to Him, and you will know the truth, and the truth will set you free, John 8:31-32.

Believe in Him, and you will have eternal life, John 3:16.

Believe in Him, and He will send the Holy Spirit, John 15:26.

Seek His kingdom righteousness, and He will give everything you need, Matthew 6:33.

Abide in Him, and you will bear much fruit, John 15:5.

Follow Him, and He will be with you to the end of the age, Matthew 28:20.

Follow Him, and He will come back for you, Revelation 22:12-13.

GUARANTEED RESULTS

These are just a short list of the promises of Jesus. Now, I don't know about you, but I've had promises broken. I've had well-meaning loved ones offer me ice cream if I'll be good in the store and then break that promise when they found out they didn't have enough money after shopping was done.

I'm not bitter.

I just want people to say what they mean and mean what they say. Ice cream is too important to bandy words and give false promises. I'm sure when the promise was made, it was meant. The problem arose when the person didn't have the power to fulfill the promise. If they didn't have the ability to do what they said they would do, I am disappointed.

When Peter writes about the promises given, he uses a word that denotes a self-committal. In other words, God is committing Himself to carry through on the promises He is giving. I've got to ask myself two questions.

1. Is He trustworthy?
2. Is He capable?

See how important it is that Peter begins by talking about the Power and the Person behind the Promises? What kind of power does God have? Godly dynamite. What has it already granted to us? Everything that helps us live a life devoted to Him. Who is He to make that promise? Just look at His reputation and His character.

He is capable.

He is trustworthy.

These are Promises of results. This isn't a human being hoping to fulfill a promise made in the heat of a shopping spree to make us behave (well, maybe I'm a little bitter). This is God, the Father, King of the Universe. He has all power at His disposal and is trustworthy and true.

> *And I am sure of this, that He who began a good work in you will bring it to completion at the day of Jesus Christ.*
> *— Philippians 1:6*

These are Promises of results designed to save your soul, make you whole, and bring you to life. These are Promises of results that bring about in you the life of grace that allows you to bless others and share The Way.

Just how amazing are those Promises? Peter tells us in the rest of the sentence.

> *. . . who called us to His own glory and excellence, by which He has granted to us His precious and very great promises,*
> *— 2 Peter 1:3-4*

- **Precious** – *timios*, recognized value, beheld as of great price.
- **Very great** – *megas*, large, great, wide, vast. As in "megalodon" or "megachurch".

Peter is reduced to using the language of a child to describe these Promises. They are so priceless that we can't comprehend it. They are so awesome that all the money in the world wouldn't be enough. To say people will recognize the value of these Promises is like saying they would recognize the value of a quadrillion dollars. How much is a quadrillion dollars? How many fast food value meals can you get with that? It's a number we can't even imagine.

It's like a kid just said he wanted a bazillion ice cream cones.

Any time our English language is reduced to using two adjectives that mean much the same thing, very and great, to describe how very great something is . . . Let's just say my English teacher in high school would have thrown up her hands. Can't you think of a better word? Magnificent? Unbelievable? Something?

As children, we are overwhelmed by something we can't explain. We see the Great Plains and they seem to go on forever. We see Big Sky country and we think we are going to fall off the earth into eternity. That's what this word means. So wide and expansive, so amazing, so *very great* that it seems to cover everything.

Talk about some cool Promises.

PUTTING PUZZLE PIECES TOGETHER

Maybe we just wore you out. You're wondering if this whole thing is too much for you to understand. Or maybe you get it, and you're tired of waiting for me to get to the point. All of these things are important because I know you have the same problem I do.

I don't have enough power to be what God is calling me to be.

I don't know if I have enough faith to be what God is calling me to be.

I don't trust promises.

Inherently, I know the idea of following Jesus, being a true disciple(maker), is a daunting task. It's why I struggle so much when I read discipleship books. I'm not sure I'm going to be equal to the task. That's a lie. I know I'm not equal to the task. Are you in the same place?

Good.

Because that's what God wants from the disciple(maker) s of His Son.

What we think of as a limitation, God sees as the beginning place. We thought our failures and imperfections were a blockade against this kind of life. God sees them as opportunities for others to see His grace. Who we were didn't stop Him from offering us the grace of salvation. Who we are doesn't stop Him from offering us a life of grace.

But He knows us better than we know ourselves. He knows we need to have an ace in the hole, a trump card, a sure thing. If we know going forward we're going to fail, what is the incentive to keep going? We need to know we're going to succeed and stop looking at the little defeats along the way as the end of the war.

Look at the end of the Bible. God wins. If God wins, we win. If we win, the war is a formality. If the war is a formality, the only thing this current battle is good for is making us better soldiers.

So He promises we already have all we need.

His divine power (godly dynamite) has granted to us (bestowed upon us, given to us) all things (not some things, not most things, not a few things) pertaining to life (mental, emotional, physical, social, spiritual) and godliness (devoting all our components of life to Him), through the knowledge of Him who called us to His own glory (His reputation, what He has done) and excellence (His character, His goodness beyond measure), by which He has granted to us (bestowed upon us, given to us) His precious (priceless, a bazillion) and very great (wide, expansive, covering everything) promises (of results).

Because He has the Power and because He is the Person who can be trusted, we can trust the Promises of eternal life, Spirit life, bearing fruit, becoming a disciple(maker) of Jesus.

We can be this, you and me.

PART 3

LIVE

HEART:
We Need to Talk First

See what God is saying here? Not your power, His. Not empty promises, real. Not by some fallible human being but by Him. All of this I've known for a long time, but for some reason I've only applied it to myself.

I was a sinner, a recovered alcoholic, who made a life of missing the mark with God. Even if I don't consider the teaching of Jesus in Matthew 5 that sins of the heart are as bad as sinful actions, I've only left one commandment unbroken. If no one had told me about His grace, I would have made the most of my life but died owing the penalty of my crimes against others.

I lied, cheated, stole. I hated, abused, berated. I amused myself with pleasures of flesh and substances and all manner of mind games. Ask anyone in my life at the time and they would have said I was a good person. Despite my actions, I was able to maintain what I now call a "hopeful reputation."

I've heard the "hopeful reputation" and often even used it for people myself. He's a drug addict, but if you knew him, you'd think he was a good guy. He's got anger issues, but he'd give you the shirt off his back. He hits his wife sometimes, but you can tell he really loves her. She never pays you back, but she's always there for the kids. She will lie right to your face, but her heart is gold. The "hopeful reputation" is what we give people to reconcile our love for them despite their shortcomings.

If this wasn't a natural, human thing to do, none of us would ever get along. The danger of it is that we excuse the sin with the good as long as we believe the good outweighs the bad. Only when we realize the good doesn't excuse the bad can we understand the grace of Jesus.

Suppose I went out and robbed a bank today. I was so clever, I got away with it. Now I have all this money, and I only need so much to survive—besides, suddenly spending a bunch of money will look suspicious. Instead, as I drive around in my beat-up Chevy mini-van (we call it The Beastie), I see a homeless guy and give him $200. I go by the shelter and rescue three dogs, then give them as pets to some kids whose parents don't mind. I find out one of those families is struggling with a medical bill and pay it for them. I go to the gym that night, and one of the ladies working there is being abused, so I give her some money to help her get away from the creep hitting her. I decide to tape anonymous envelopes on all the local charities, each with a thousand dollars in it, to help them take care of other people.

The next morning, I wake up, and the SWAT team is kicking in my door. They've found me out. As they cuff me, I say, "No, wait, you don't understand! I'm basically a good person! I've helped puppies and kids and abused women and homeless people and given lots of money to charity!" The officers won't care. I'm still guilty of the crime, and now that I'm caught, I will answer for it.

God feels the same way about sin.

He's not being mean to us if He holds us accountable for what we've done to break our relationship with Him, hurt people, and hurt ourselves. He is not discounting all the great things we've done in the meantime. He's simply enforcing the law. We broke it; now we must pay for it—that's justice. When we realize this is what He is doing, we can either feel belligerent about it and protest His right to arrest and condemn us, or we can finally let our shoulders slump and admit we've been in the wrong. Our reaction doesn't matter. God will be just anyway.

The great thing about God is grace. It's the heart of His truth. When we finally admit we are wrong, He then shows us that He is willing to take the penalty for our crime. His Son dies for us, which relieves us of the penalty. Not fair, no. Grace.

But then Jesus rises again. Conquers death. That's Power. Power enough to grant us eternal life and all the other Promises. Now, I can hold my head up and believe in Him, knowing should I fail again He has already paid the penalty. He promised me, and He has never lied, never forsaken me, never left me. His reputation and character guarantee me what I need to be free.

115

That's a lot to take in, but I feel like I've got that part now. I'm getting better at remembering it when I mess up. I still feel guilty when I do, but I no longer feel like I should punish myself for it. I believe in God's grace for me in my salvation.

My new struggle is understanding why. Why did He do this for me and then leave me here?

It's time to ask a different question. What is in it for Him?

So that . . .

That question didn't come easily for me. Much of my Christian life was spent asking what was in it for me. How can it make me a better person? How can I have a better marriage? How can my kids turn out okay? How can I repair my finances?

I listened to sermons, even prepared sermons, trying to wade through the first thirty minutes to get to the action list. What are the things I can do to improve me? It's confusing, too, because some of those things seem altruistic. Giving helps my pastor keep his job and allows us to do events. Serving helps others enjoy Sunday morning. Teaching increases the knowledge of those willing to be students. Attending events gives satisfaction to those who plan them.

All of these are things I've done that help other people even as I was focused on me. I want to be a better Christian, have a better reputation, run in a better circle of friends, have a better family, and retire in a better home. I never meant to be a selfish

Christian. Most people in my church would have laughed if someone called me a selfish Christian.

I was, though.

Not only that, I berated those who didn't follow in my footsteps. People who felt they were basically good enough now that salvation had fixed the whole hell problem. What's the big deal? I love Jesus, and that's enough, right? Don't bother us with all the rules and stuff because we live under grace now. Listen to the pastor. Just last week, he told us if we wanted to grow in Christ, we had to read our Bibles, pray, and attend church. I've done all three this week! I get plenty of Scripture from the sermon. I talk to God all the time! I'm here, ain't I?

No, no, no, you don't get it. If you do all these other things, you will be even more blessed! But what if I don't really care about being more blessed? Is that why God saved me so that He could ask me to do all these extra things and bless me more because of it?

What's the "so that" in this?

Everything God does has a purpose. Everything written about God in the Scriptures has a purpose. That's why we see *therefore* used so often in the Bible, why so often there's a *for* or a *since* in the language. We can't go very far without seeing one of those phrases that tell us why we needed to know the last thing we were told. One of my theology professors once told our class when we saw a *therefore* in Scripture, we needed to look at what preceded it and ask what it is there for.

I hate ending sentences in a preposition. It's the writer in me.

Anyway, another phrase the Bible translators use to get this idea across is *so that*. When we see that phrase, it usually means something was just explained for a purpose. What follows is the purpose. Here's what we have so far:

> *His divine power has granted to us all things that pertain to life and godliness, through the knowledge of Him who called us to His own glory and excellence, by which He has granted to us His precious and very great promises, so that . . .*
>
> — *2 Peter 1:3-4 (emphasis mine)*

See it? There's a reason all this has been done for us. The Power, the Person, and the Promises are all given to us for a reason. I think Peter tries to convey to us just how much that affects him by the way he begins this letter. Take a look at the greeting at the beginning of this letter.

> *Simeon Peter, a servant and apostle of Jesus Christ . . .*
>
> — *2 Peter 1:1*

He's not addressing himself as Peter, the Rock, the one Christ gave a name and the keys to the Kingdom. Before that, he was Simeon, the fisherman, the doubter, the work-a-day, blue-collar guy who didn't give much thought to priestly things. He's not just an apostle of Jesus Christ, a messenger, one of the Twelve, a leader of leaders in the church. Before that, he saw himself as a servant, a slave, someone unworthy of the calling to follow this man Jesus and even betraying Him when it seemed to matter most.

Simeon is a Middle with a tendency toward impulse. He's been given a new name and a position of importance, but it doesn't change the fact that he still feels unworthy and is no one special in the scheme of things. Without God's Power, Person, and Promises, he's just an ordinary guy. But God . . .

Now, Simeon, the servant is Peter the Apostle, but God has given him those things for a purpose.

SO THAT WE MAY BECOME...

The Purpose of the Person with the Power giving us the Promises is that we may become. The word used here in the Greek means to emerge, to transition from one point to another. It can mean to be born.

In Matthew 5:43-45, Jesus tells us we must love and pray for people who wish evil on us instead of hating them as the world would tell us to hate them. Why? So that we can emerge as, be born as, and transition into becoming sons of our Father in Heaven.

In Matthew 18:3, Jesus says we must emerge as, be born as, and transition into becoming like little children. Why? It's the only way to enter the Kingdom of Heaven.

In John 12:35-36, Jesus says while He is with the disciples, they are to believe in Him. Why? To emerge as, be born as, and transition into becoming like Him. (Especially poignant to us if we consider He promises in Matthew 18:20 to be with us always.)

In John 15:8, Jesus says God will be glorified if we bear much fruit. Why? Because it will prove that we are emerging as, born as, transitioning into becoming the disciple(maker)s of Jesus.

Don't miss this process. We love people differently, innocently as children, believing in Jesus and bearing fruit because it proves there is a new us, created in grace to live in grace. Jesus throughout His life teaches us that living in grace is what allows us to bear fruit. Since that is the case,

> *Do all things without grumbling or disputing, so that you may become (emerge as, be born as, transition into becoming) blameless and innocent, children of God without blemish, in the midst of a crooked generation, among whom you will shine as lights in the world, holding fast to the word of life . . .*
>
> *— Philippians 2:14-16 (with my addition)*

Not so that we may do. So that we may become. Emerge. Be reborn. Transition. Know the Person with the Power is giving you Promises so that you can be. Being is better than doing. Anyone can do a kind thing. But kindness is a different thing altogether. Anyone can do a good deed. But being a good person? Try that for a day. If we don't have the Person and the Power and the Promises, it's impossible.

But with God, all things are possible.

SO THAT WE MAY BECOME PARTAKERS...

In my time as a believer, I've been a part of about a dozen churches. Among those churches, I would reckon half had either a Sunday school class, a small group, or a social get-together called *Koinonia.*

It's a great Greek word that is used often in the Bible and is translated "fellowship." It sounds cool, and it's even more fun to say. KOY-NO-NEE-AH. Say it ten times real fast. I get the warm and fuzzies.

I'm also warmed by the concept. It's why we use it in our churches so much. It is a feminine word (I'm talking about the syntax, not any reference to gender) in the Greek and deals with relationships. When we think of potluck dinners, bean suppers, variety shows, women's fellowships, men's retreats, all the things that bring the church together and help build friendships among our people, we are building *koinonia.*

Every time I see something that alludes to this word, I think of those great events that are largely inward-focused and are more about the church loving the church than anything else. These events are right and good and should not be neglected by even the most evangelistic pastors. People need to belong. It helps them believe.

When I looked at this passage in the second letter of Peter and saw the word *partakers*, the pretend Greek scholar in me immediately thought, "Oh! I bet that's KOY-NO-NEE-AH!" (At which time I said it ten times real fast.) I looked it up and was rewarded with the word *koinonos* and almost stopped reading. I knew it! I was right! All this stuff about the Power and the Promises of the Person leads us to potluck meals, Sunday School classes, and fellowship retreats!

But my eyes caught the word "masculine" in the description. Wait. What?

Turns out there is a difference between *koinonia* and *koinonos*. The first one is about relationship, but the second one has a different meaning behind it.

- *Koinonia* is relational and represents a participant who belongs to a fellowship but is largely focused on the benefit to each person.
- *Koinonos* is more about the function and focuses on the fellowship as a whole. It's a participant of something larger than themselves that is not focused on them.

Peter is purposefully drawing a distinction here. The Person with the Power didn't give us the Promises for us to focus on ourselves and reap the benefits. Oh, He wants that all right. He loves *koinonia* as much as we do. But Peter is letting us know that the Purpose is greater than what it does for us. We are joining into something much greater than ourselves. What is it?

PARTAKERS OF THE DIVINE NATURE

The phrase that describes what we are joining uses the same word as before for divine. Godly. This refers to God's separateness and our natural devotion. The other word is nature and is only used in a handful of places in New Testament books.

In Romans, Paul is talking about the circumcised. By this, he means the Jews who have been born of the covenant and bear the mark of the covenant. He also talks about the uncircumcised, by which he means those not born under the covenant—the Gentiles—and includes everyone who is not Jewish. He's making the point that neither Jews nor Gentiles are exonerated from following God's guidelines for living, and neither of them has been capable of following them without failing. In fact, those outside the covenant are sometimes better at it than those inside the covenant!

> *Then he who is physically uncircumcised but keeps the law will condemn you who have the written code and circumcision but break the law.*
>
> — *Romans 2:27 (emphasis mine)*

This passage is an interesting study for Bible nerds, but for the moment, I want to draw attention to the word "physically." Paul is talking about people who, in their physical nature, haven't committed to the law of God. This is in their body, not in theory. They have a physical nature that is different from the others—where Jews are circumcised physically, Gentiles are physically uncircumcised. The same concept is in Peter's passage, but it denotes an even greater difference.

Divine physical nature—a part of the blueprint, the DNA, if you will, of God. When God, through Peter, wants us to understand why He gave us the Power and the Promises, He tells us it's to be part of something larger than ourselves: God's very nature.

We take part in what makes God God.

Now, don't take this too far and start saying God is in all of us and in everything and belittle the truth being presented here. I'm not saying all is God, and God is all. I'm saying those who trust the Person for grace are Promised the Power to Partake in that nature. We get to be a part of Who He is, not just what He is doing.

If I'm going to be a part of God, I want to know what it means to "partake" in it. Don't you? I looked at some places where this other form of fellowship is used in the Bible.

In Matthew 23:29-30, Jesus says if the Pharisees had been alive when their ancestors were killing prophets, they would have *taken part* in killing them. This gives us a sense of participation.

In 1 Corinthians 10:20, Paul says when people worship something other than God, he doesn't want us to be *participants* in it. This gives us a sense of association.

In 2 Corinthians 1:7, Paul says that as the church *participates* in the sufferings of Paul, they will also *participate* in the comfort he has found. This gives us a sense of sharing something intimate.

In 2 Corinthians 8:23, Paul says Titus is his *partner* and co-laborer for the benefit of the church. This gives a sense that it is more than just working alongside someone to accomplish something. This is a partnership.

Finally, in Luke 5:9-10, Luke describes the relationship between Simeon Peter and the two sons of Zebedee as *partners* with him. This gives us a sense that they are business partners who share the risk and the reward of their ventures.

To be a partaker is to be someone who associates with something in an intimate, sharing way that makes them partners who share the risks and rewards. Co-owners, collaborators, vested partners. This is deeper than just a relational connection. This is a deep bond that shares the outcome of an endeavor. The Purpose.

The Person with the Power who gave us those Promises gave them so that we would become intimate, vested Partners in God's mission because we share God's nature and thereby have the desire to see His Purpose succeed. And what is His Purpose?

> *Now, after John was arrested, Jesus came into Galilee, proclaiming the Gospel of God and saying, "The time is fulfilled, and the Kingdom of Heaven is at hand; repent and believe in the Gospel."*
>
> — *Mark 1:14-15*

From the very beginning of His teaching, Jesus focuses on our citizenship in the Kingdom of God. He is the Messiah, the

Anointed One, the King, and come to reclaim earth through His life (the Son), His death (the Savior), and His resurrection (proof that He is God). While He was on this earth, He led the disciple(maker)s. After His ascension into heaven, He left Peter and the other believers to spread the Word: Repent (rethink) and put your faith in (give your allegiance to) Jesus of Nazareth, and you will be saved, empowered, and set loose on the mission (through the Holy Spirit) to make more disciple(maker)s.

Disciple-making is for God because He has made us more than Plan A. He has made us the only plan. Jesus dies and rises again, conquering death and asking us to believe. When we do, He sends us to find more of His kids. There is no Plan B.

Disciple-making is for us because we are dead without Him. He pays the penalty for our crimes Himself and asks us to trust Him for it. When we do, He sends us to find more of His kids.

Disciple-making is for them because we were once them. They don't know what we know—that the day is coming when the penalty will need to be paid, and they can't pay it.

For we ourselves were once foolish, disobedient, led astray, slaves to various passions and pleasures, passing our days in malice and envy, hated by others and hating one another. But when the goodness and lovingkindness of God our Savior appeared, He saved us, not because of works done by us in righteousness, but according to His own mercy, by the washing of regeneration and renewal of the Holy Spirit, whom He poured out on us richly through Jesus Christ our savior, so that being justified by His grace we might become heirs according to the hope of eternal life. The saying is trustworthy, and I want you to insist on these things, so that those who have believed in God may be careful to devote themselves to good works. These things are excellent and profitable for people.

— *Titus 3:3-8*

Disciple-making is for God, for us, for them.

For God, for Type-A's, for Others.

For God, for Middles, for the people around them.

For God, for Not Yets, for Already Believers.

At The Jar, we say we are filled by the Spirit to be emptied for others.

Feeling overwhelmed still? I've got more Good News.

WHAT'S IN OUR WAY?

I still think like a Middle.

Something is bugging me about all this. I mean, if everything that's been said so far is true, then why hasn't the world been set on fire? Are we that off in our preaching and teaching? I don't think so. Most of the thoughts recorded here can be found in other places. This isn't earth-shattering news to believers already, is it? All we've done is explore the Good News, the Great Commandments, and the Great Commission and conclude that we're empowered to be disciple(maker)s of Jesus who make disciple(maker)s of Jesus.

Surprise, surprise.

No, that's not the surprise. The surprise is how few are living it out. Isn't that why we have so many disciple-making books today? Everyone is trying to delve into the psyche of average Christians and get them to wake up? If most of us know all this, why aren't most of us driven to live like this?

Well, I think it is sin.

No, I don't mean Christians are just as corrupt as the next person. And I don't mean we let our current sinful actions keep us lazy or unfruitful or ineffective. That may be true for some of us, but most who feel that way are the Others, the ten percent who won't become disciple(maker)s no matter what they are taught.

I'm talking about the way sin keeps Type-A's running around chaotically trying to measure up and Middles sitting in the pews and chairs at church. I'm talking about the way we feel about our sin as much as what sins we commit. There's something insidious about sin that gets in our way. We feel guilty, sure, when we do something wrong. Repentance (rethinking) is all we need to cure that. What is repentance? Remembering the penalty is paid, rethinking how God wants us to live, and turning back to God for forgiveness and guidance. We can do that with each individual sin. What I'm talking about is how all those sins add up to something stronger than guilt.

SHAME, SHAME, SHAME

In the two decades that I have been in full-time ministry, I've dealt with my fair share of addicts. I don't have much formal training for that, so I let them know right away that I am not a counselor or a psychologist. I'm sure every addict has a story about how they got into their mess. I'm just not qualified to wade into their mess and fix that.

A counselor delves into the past to fix the present so we can have hope in the future. I can't do that, partly because I'm not good at it and partly because I'm not licensed. What I can do is delve into the present to fix the present so we can have hope for the future. It's amazing how often I talk to a person who has been through rehab and counseling and can use therapy terms to describe their mother's abuse, their father's absence, their unfortunate circumstance, their stupid choice, but still can't kick the habit.

They know all about what happened in the past to make them susceptible. They've been told to forgive themselves and the person who hurt them. They've been told to let go of the past so they can enjoy the present. They've been told the cause of their pain and why they seek solace. All those things are amazing remedies for the soul. I'm for them. I believe in them. I think everyone should have a little therapy to get in touch with why they are where they are.

Sometimes, an addict will get what is needed from these sessions and start fresh for a new life. When this doesn't help the addict, though, he begins to lose hope. When the past has been confronted but the addiction remains, she begins to think she will never be free. I think I know one reason why.

The addict has begun to identify with the addiction.

They say things like, "I'm a drug addict."

They blame all their decisions on the drug.

They excuse themselves from trying to get clean because the addiction won't let them.

When I'm dealing with an addict, the first thing I ask is, "So, did you choose the drug, or did the drug choose you?" I do this for two reasons. First, I want to find out how they got into using in the first place. It's a great way to open up some questions about the past from the beginning of the problem instead of looking further back for other problems. After all, by the time an addict comes to me, they've explored all that.

But the second reason is more important than the first. I want them to start thinking of the drug as separate from the person. I want them to stop identifying with the drug and start creating an identity separate from it. I am not a drug addict. I am a person who has become hooked on drugs.

When I am the drug, I am ashamed to admit it. My shame actually keeps me from believing I can do anything about it. "I'd love to get clean, but my drug (my shame) won't let me." That's different than, "I'd love to get clean; how can I separate myself from the drug?" (Can you hear the similarity to our conversation about strongholds?)

When someone tries to use shame to deflect my help, I ask, "Is that you or the addiction talking?"

We don't think of sin as addiction because society tells us addiction is different. Addiction involves substances, websites, habits that are detrimental to society, and things people can't help choosing to do even though they know it's wrong, and they respond to correction by getting angry, frustrated, and bitter.

Yep. Sounds like sin to me.

Sometimes sin includes substances like money, time, relationships. Sometimes, sin includes websites like shopping (spending money we don't have), computer games (spending time we don't have), and relationships (experiencing relationships without the hassle of sharing our lives).

What is sin but habits that are detrimental to society? When is thieving, lying, adultery, or envy ever good for us or the people around us? Aren't they sometimes things we feel we've lost control over? We know they are wrong for us, but we choose to do them anyway.

How do we respond when someone points out our sin? Like an addict! We get angry and tell them they are worse than we are. We get frustrated and tell them we're doing our best, but we're not perfect. We get bitter and cut off relationships.

Addiction is the visible sin, but sin in all its forms trucks in guilt and shame. God gave us guilt, the red light on our dashboard that keeps us from repeating mistakes. We own shame all by ourselves.

SINFUL ACTS VS. SINFUL NATURE

Even the most devout believers, true disciples of Jesus, have a sin addiction. Something they are doing feels like it has control over them. (If you've been paying attention, now you're *really* thinking of strongholds). They know they shouldn't do it, but they do it anyway. Often, when they commit this sin, they do what they think is right and good. They punish themselves. After all, God wants them to be perfect. Right?

Except God already paid for that sin before you ever committed it. Here's a good exercise. List on a piece of paper every sin you committed before Jesus rose from the grave. Go ahead. Use a couple of sheets if you need them. How many sins did you commit before Jesus paid for them?

Zero. Everyone came after the penalty was paid. So why are you so intent on punishing yourself for something God already suffered to erase? If you think you are alone in doing this, consider Paul. This guy who wrote much of the New Testament struggled with it, too! The seventh chapter of his letter to Romans talks about it.

> *For I do not understand my actions. For I do not do what I want, but I do the very thing I hate. Now if I do what I do not want, I agree with the law, that it is good.*
> — *Romans 7:15-16*

When he sins, he hates it and can't get past the fact that he is agreeing with the law that he is guilty. God wants us to recognize this in us because it proves our need for salvation. But He doesn't want us to be ashamed and withdraw from Him. He wants to heal that for us.

> *So now it is no longer I who do it, but sin that dwells within me. For I know that nothing good dwells in me, that is, in my flesh. For I have the desire to do what is right, but not the ability to carry it out. For I do not do the good I want, but the evil I do not want is what I keep on doing. Now if I do what I do not want, it is no longer I who do it, but sin that dwells within me.*
> — *Romans 7:17-20*

We've talked about this in previous volumes (remember, in *Follow*, I warned you we would see repetitions in the teaching). Paul is describing what it feels like to live under the Law, not how it feels to walk in the Spirit (see Romans 8). However, if we aren't careful, *shame* will bring us back here under the Law to live. Before Jesus, we did bad things because we were the kind of people who do bad things. After Jesus, we are not the kind of people who do bad things, but sometimes we make those mistakes anyway.

When I sin as a believer, I want to do what is right, but I don't have the will to carry it out. So when I rely on myself to behave, I fall. Paul tells us this is sin in us, dwelling in us, causing us to do what we don't want to do. I am fighting my adversary, my old man, for control of my body. My daddy calls it "The Black Irish" or "The Dark Man." Any time I rely on my own power, I fall into this trap.

My addiction becomes me, and I become my addiction.

But when I recognize that I am not sin, I am free from the shame of being sin because I am no longer identified by it. Have you ever noticed how often Christians go around calling themselves sinners saved by grace? "I'm just an unworthy sinner, and I'm never going to be more than that. Good thing Jesus loves me because I sure don't deserve it."

What?

Then why is it that Paul doesn't start his letters by addressing them to sinners? If this is proper theology, to be identified with my sin, why doesn't he write to the sinners in Ephesus and Colossae and Corinth. Especially to Corinth! Have you seen all the crazy things happening in that church? One guy was sleeping with his father's wife! But that's not how Paul addresses them despite their continued sin.

To all those in Rome who are loved by God and called to be saints: Grace to you and peace from God our Father and the Lord Jesus Christ.

— Romans 1:7

To the church of God that is in Corinth, to those sanctified in Christ Jesus, called to be saints together with all those who in every place call upon the name of our Lord Jesus Christ, both their Lord and ours . . .

— 1 Corinthians 1:2

To the saints who are in Ephesus, and are faithful in Christ Jesus.

— Ephesians 1:1

To all the saints in Christ Jesus who are at Philippi, with the overseers and deacons . . .

— Philippians 1:1

To the saints and faithful brothers in Christ at Colossae . . .

— Colossians 1:2

Saints. Sanctified. Faithful. That's how we are identified by God. We are not our sin. We've been cleaned out. We are already what He wants us to be, but we are not yet all that He wants us to be. God has finished His work through Christ, but He has not finished His work in us. Go back to that passage in Peter's second letter and pick up something we left out in the last chapter.

We *may become* partakers of the divine nature. Already, by virtue of the sacrifice of Jesus, we are made perfect when we believe in Him (For our sake He made Him to be sin Who knew no sin, so that in Him we might become the righteousness of God – 2 Corinthians 5:21), but we are not yet living in grace perfectly as our Rabbi did while He was on this earth.

Why?

Because by leaving us here, we can accomplish two things for Him. First, we can prove the validity of the Good News by exhibiting the change in us when we are saved. Second, we can spread the Good News by exhibiting the changes in us after we are saved. To be effective and fruitful, though, we must believe in the Power of the Person who Promised us we could Partake in His divine nature to accomplish His Purpose. We need to live in grace when it comes to sin as well as when it comes to good deeds.

Sounding like borderline heresy

I know what some of you Type-A's are thinking—that everyone should be as steeped in doctrine as you are. We all need a little Greek in our lives, right? Relax, I'm a Middle but I'm also a Bible nerd. I'm not saying our sin doesn't matter. I agree with Paul when he wrote:

> *What shall we say, then? Are we to continue in sin that grace may abound? By no means! How can we who died to sin still live in it?*
>
> *— Romans 6:1-2*

I'm not advocating a free lifestyle that takes advantage of the grace of God. No cheap grace here. What I'm saying is we still sin sometimes (that's guilt), but we are not identified with our sin any longer (that's shame). Our identity is in Christ.

We. Are. Saints.

That's tough if you've never thought of it that way. Saints? Isn't that reserved for really holy guys and gals who did extraordinary things for God? Patrick? Francis? Brigid? Teresa? Elizabeth? Not according to Paul. According to his inspired writing, all the believers in the church were saints.

You are, too.

Yes, you are.

Don't argue with me.

Stop thinking of "saint" as a description of your holiness, and start thinking of it as a description of your position in Christ. Sin no longer has sway over you because you are not sin's property anymore. You are Christ's. When Jesus died for you, He not only cured your sinful acts, He also cured your sinful nature.

> *So I find it to be a law that when I want to do right, evil lies close at hand. For I delight in the law of God, in my inner being, but I see in my members another law waging war against the law of my mind and making me captive to the law of sin that dwells in my members.*
>
> *— Romans 7:21-23*

Paul recognizes the fight is not over. Grace has set us free, but sin—a separate law, a separate entity—is still trying to get the best of us. The addiction is talking. We decide if we should listen to it, but we no longer identify with it. So even when we fail, we already know the outcome.

Wretched man that I am! Who will deliver me from this body of death? Thanks be to God through Jesus Christ our Lord! So then, I myself serve the Law of God with my mind, but with my flesh I serve the law of sin.
— Romans 7:24-25

We'll get to this idea of "flesh" in a later chapter in the next section. For now, suffice to say that we, like animals, want to live in the here and now for what most attracts, pleases, or meets a survival need. My dog Neville loves me—I believe that—but he never loves me more than when I have a bag of Cheetos. Oh, how he loves Cheetos and me!

In that order.

When we are confronted with an opportunity to become a more devoted disciple(maker) of Jesus Christ, our sin starts talking to us. Sin tells us all about our past and why it's too late to make that decision. Sin tells us we're too defiled, too weak, too dark, too corrupted to make that decision. Sin tells us we are not worthy. That's a stronghold because that is not what God thinks. We sometimes forget that and let ourselves think we might be saved, but we are just sinners in the hands of a God of grace. Only . . .

There is therefore now no condemnation for those who are in Christ Jesus. For the law of the Spirit of life has set you free in Christ Jesus from the law of sin and death.
— Romans 8:1-2 (emphasis mine)

Do you see it? *Therefore…*

The point of the passage isn't that we are sinful. All Paul said about how we feel about living a holy life and finding ourselves sinning over and over again? That was taught *so that* we could come to a conclusion. We are not sinners anymore. We are saints, no longer condemned but set free, no longer searching but finding our identity in Christ.

I'm not preaching the heresy of complacency when it comes to obedience. I'm preaching against the stronghold of feeling unsaved, unworthy, and unloved by God because we aren't perfect. That wasn't true when we were saved at the beginning, and it's not true now. If we grasp this, we will be ready to face sin for what it is.

THE ENEMY

I'm not taking anything away from Satan here, not discounting him, but sin is what separates us from God, not Satan. Although Satan is an adversary, his only power is to deceive us or tempt us to commit sin or to accuse us of the sin we've already committed. Hollywood has given him too much credit.

As a believer, I am armored against him and his attacks. I need only put on the full armor of God to be prepared for him (Ephesians 6:13-20). But sin is the tool he uses to keep us from being effective and fruitful in our ministry. He wants us focused on ourselves, so he pushes us toward sin. When we sin, so much happens inside us that we have a hard time seeing outside ourselves.

St. John-of-the-Cross understood this when he wrote a book called *The Ascent on Mt. Carmel*. He wrote it to give spiritual direction to those who would be disciple(maker)s of Jesus. I don't agree with everything he wrote (I don't *understand* everything he wrote!), but I do get this. Sin creates the following in us:

1. **Weariness of Soul.** We get satisfaction for a moment, but we need more and more. It's like throwing a log on the fire, except the fire increases even when the fuel runs out. Think of addiction—the user always needs a bigger hit, a more potent drug. Sin is the same way. *As when a hungry man dreams, and behold, he is eating and awakes with his hunger not satisfied (Isaiah 29:8).*

2. **Torment of Soul.** We are haunted by what we've done, but we can't seem to stop. We feel like a part of us has been stolen by the poor choice we've made, and we are right. My opportunities become limited by the consequences of my sin. *My wounds stink and fester because of my foolishness, I am utterly bowed down and prostrate (Psalm 38:5-6; the entire Psalm speaks of this condition).*

3. **Darkness of Soul.** Our desire for something not God burns so darkly, that it blots out the light of His grace. We can't let ourselves be in the light because then He

will know. *For evils have encompassed me beyond num-ber; my iniquities have overtaken me, and I cannot see (Psalm 40:12).*

4. **Defiling of Soul.** Living for sin instead of God is like drinking mud instead of water. It's not just that the mud is worse; very little mud can ruin a perfectly good glass of the purest water. *They wandered, blind, through the streets; they were so defiled with blood that no one was able to touch their garments (Lamentations 4:14; the whole chapter captures this thought).*

5. **Weakness of Soul.** If all that weren't bad enough, sin has a cumulative effect. When we sin, we are weaker the next time sin crouches at our door. Over time, no devil has to whisper in our ear. We are tempted enough by our own voice to stray from His way. *For the desires of the flesh are against the Spirit, and the desires of the Spirit are against the flesh, for these are opposed to each other, to keep you from doing the things you want to do (Galatians 5:17).*

Weary, tormented, dark, defiled, and weak, we struggle to raise our heads and give homage to the God who saved us.

Unless we fall on the mercy of grace for our guilt *and our shame.* Unless we understand the beauty of what He has done for us, once and for all, to cover every sin past, present, and future. Unless we get it that He is not lording over us our imperfection but covering that imperfection with His perfection.

MORE THAN CONQUERORS

So do this exercise for me. In Appendix A, at the back of this book are most of the sins as outlined in the New Testament. They have their name, the Greek word (for Bible nerds), and what the sin looks like. First are sins that hurt us as individuals (though because of that, they hurt others), and on the page behind it are sins that hurt the people around us (though because of that, they hurt us). What I want you to do is go through each list and circle the ones that you have committed during your lifetime.

Then I want you to go back and put a star next to the ones you can't help repeating.

Go on. No one is looking. If you are doing this with a group of people, go somewhere they can't see what you are putting down. This isn't about someone else telling you what you are guilty of doing. This is about trying to recognize where shame is living in your soul. Now that you've starred the ones you often do put a big square around the ones that most often bring you shame.

Shame is the feeling that this sin has so wearied, tormented, darkened, defiled, and weakened you that you've started believing you are no longer disciple-making material. That sin? That's your stronghold.

Ready, set, go.

Are you done? Okay, now I want you to do me a favor. I want you to rip those pages out of your book. I mean it. Rip it out. No, really. I know you love books, and you might want to keep the book intact to remember what you learned. I promise you, the frayed ends of where this page is enough of a reminder. Rip it out.

Now, I want you to open your Bible to Psalm 51. I mean it. Go get a Bible. I'd rather you didn't use your phone because your hands are going to be busy. Get a real, printed version of the Bible and open it up to Palm 51. If you are leading a group, open to Psalm 51 and get ready to read it for them.

Okay. You should have the Bible open to Psalm 51, and you should have the two pages of sins from this book in your hands. Now, I want you to turn the pages sideways so that the sentences are traveling from bottom to top instead of left to right. Rip the pages down the middle. Go ahead, rip them. You should now have two half-pages in each hand.

Try to put the two pieces of each page back together. Use tape if you want, but it won't work. No matter what you do, you can no longer put those pages back together. It is forever less than it was before you ripped it.

That's what sin does to you. It causes your relationship with God, your relationship with people, and your relationship with yourself to be split and broken, irreparable.

Hold those separate pieces, two in each hand. Now, ball each one up into your fists so that you have a tiny crumpled mess of paper in each hand. Don't just hold it, squeeze it. Squeeze it hard. Squeeze it like you intend never to let it go.

This is the stronghold of shame. Recognizing our sin and the brokenness it creates, then holding onto it so tightly that no one can get you to let it go. Do you feel the strain in your hands? Don't stop squeezing! This is what your soul feels like, holding onto sin.

Now, read aloud to yourself Psalm 51. Don't skip this step. It's the Psalm David wrote when Nathan revealed his sin with Bathsheba and Uriah. He was an adulterer, a murderer, a coward, a liar, and a creep. Read the whole Psalm. When you feel God's grace, release the paper.

Feel the release in your hands. Feel the release in your heart. God never intended you to carry the burden He took from you. No more shame. No more fear. No more sin. God has made you whole.

Take a minute and reflect.

The first time I did this exercise with a group of people, I then lit a fire in a trash can and asked people to go get their sin pages and toss them in the fire. The sin isn't just released; it's gone. Ashes. No more.

Like your sin is in the Name of Jesus.

THAT NASTY TOMATO

Ever sliced too many tomatoes on Wednesday and had to throw some of the slices in the trash? After you did, have you ever told your spouse to remember to take the trash out the next morning? Has your spouse ever forgotten?

Nearly a week later, have you accidentally knocked your keys into the trash can and heard them somehow find their path all the way to the bottom? Maybe you reached down into the can for the keys and had your fingers sink into that week-old tomato?

If you have, are you still married? Because that's real grace.

Peter tells us there is corruption in the world, but the word he uses should make you think about how gross that tomato feels after spending a week in a hot garbage can. Reading this passage and thinking of that tomato helps us understand the depth of His revulsion.

> . . . so that through them you may become partakers of the divine nature, having escaped from the corruption that is in the world because of sinful desire.
>
> — 2 Peter 1:4

The corruption is as nasty as a rotten tomato is in the world, but we have fled from it. We are no longer bearers of shame because we chose to trust Jesus to clean us and make us whole. More than that, we have come to realize this God of grace is worthy of all our desire.

The world struggles with that. They are afraid that by desiring God alone, they will miss out on some things they think they need to survive, or want to make life fun, or crave to keep the darkness at bay. They don't realize this desire for anything not God is why there is so much to survive, why life doesn't feel fun, and why darkness creeps in.

When we are saved—when we realize our disciple-making is for God, for us, for them—we stop holding onto the nasty tomato and finally flee from what the world says is okay and step into the light. We no longer worry about hiding anything. We are free.

When John wrote his first letter in the New Testament, he talked about God as light. We often think of light as goodness, but in this case, I think he was talking about transparency.

> *This is the message we have heard from Him and pro-claim to you, that God is light, and in Him is no darkness at all. If we say we have fellowship with Him while we walk in darkness, we lie and do not practice the truth. But if we walk in the light, as He is in the light, we have fellowship with one another, and the blood of Jesus His Son cleanses us from all sin.*
>
> — *1 John 1:5-7*

If John meant goodness, then the passage means that only if we walk in goodness will we have fellowship with each other and be free from sin. But that's not the Good News. No, this light is transparency. God has nothing to hide. When we trust Him, we also have nothing to hide. Our righteousness is His righteousness; our confessed sin is a tool for Him to show His grace.

Most of us will still hide our sin even though it isn't necessary. We've been conditioned by the Church to believe only perfect people can be respected. Because of this false teaching, sin has its way with many of the Already Believers and scares away the Not Yets. If we were willing to forgive each other for confessed sin the way God forgives us, healing light would come into those dark corners.

I'm not saying disciple(maker)s always tell everyone everything they ever did wrong. I'm saying times will come when your confession of a pet sin and God's grace to you that covers it will be the way He heals you of it and reaches the person in the pews struggling with the same sin. Do you know how I know this is true?

> *If we say we have no sin, we deceive ourselves, and the truth is not in us. If we confess our sins, He is faithful and just to forgive us our sins and to cleanse us from all unrighteousness.*
>
> — *1 John 1:8-9*

Don't let that nasty tomato ruin your life. Give it willingly to Him and let Him use it for His glory. Don't let sin keep you from being a disciple(maker). Remember grace is not just for your immediate salvation but also for living your life walking in the Spirit. Realize your sin as much as your understanding of God is part of your testimony to a world that isn't looking for perfect people but for a gracious Savior. God rescued you from your sin *and* your sin nature.

In other words, Middle, you are free to be a disciple(maker) once you know what it is.

WHAT A DISCIPLE(MAKER) IS

Too often, when we think of what it means to follow Jesus, we think of Paul. I have great respect for the man. God used him to bring light to the Gentiles, which means I can trace my salvation story back to him. I love Paul.

But in every town where Paul planted a church, he left behind a courageous group of people who were already behind the eight-ball. The Jews thought it was blasphemy. The authorities thought it rebellion. Even within their communities, they fought heresy. Were it not for their willingness to repent (rethink) and embrace the faith (allegiance) and fight for it, Paul's church planting would have been unsuccessful.

What about their mistakes? Without them, we would never have learned what we know about the true faith. In the letters written to encourage them, admonish them, and teach them, we have the foundation for how we do church. Paul was an amazing figure, but these are the real heroes.

Unnamed but not untested, true believers contending for the faith against all odds.

Like you and me.

A disciple(maker) is not defined by leadership or position in the church. Disciple(maker)s are defined by their willingness to look like Jesus, think like Jesus, act like Jesus, smell like Jesus as they go from day to day into their world. Disciple(maker)s know the struggle is real and need a reminder in their rearview mirrors that strengthens them when following Jesus is harder than they thought. They learn and teach Jesus as they go, not in any class or formal setting, but by living in grace, blessing others, and sharing The Way.

These things we can do, Middles. Doesn't make us better than the Type-A's, doesn't make us as unfruitful as the Others. We are the backbone, the meat, the hands and feet of Jesus. Someone else might be the mouth and the ears and such, but we are the ones ministry flows through.

How is that possible for people like us?

His (not ours) divine Power (godly dynamite) has granted to us (bestowed upon us, given to us) all things (not some things, not most things, not a few things) pertaining to life (mental, emotional, physical, social, spiritual) and godliness (devoting all our components of life to Him), through the knowledge of Him who called us to His own glory (His reputation, what He has done) and excellence (His character, His goodness beyond measure), by which He has granted to us (bestowed upon us, given to us) His precious (priceless, a bazillion) and very great (wide, expansive, covering everything) Promises (of results), so that we may become (because God has not made us all He wants us to be) Partakers (co-owners, partners, co-missionaries) of the divine nature (we are already made perfect in Him), having escaped (fled from) the corruption (that rotten tomato) that is in the world because of sinful desire (not just our sin acts but our sin nature).

— 2 Peter 1:3-4, Rogers paraphrase

Because of the ultimate Power of the Person Who, by His reputation and character, made Promises we can take to the bank:

1. We can be His disciple(maker)s because of His Spirit.
2. We are His disciple(maker)s as we go through life, not because we go somewhere special.
3. Jesus has finished His work, but through His Spirit, the Father has only one plan to bring as many of the remaining captives home as possible: our willingness to be His.
4. Being a disciple(maker) means living in grace, blessing others, and sharing The Way.

This is not above you, Middle.
This is not beneath you, Middle.
This is just for you, Middle.
Peter's letter tells us how to prepare.

SOUL:
Faith and Virtue

You've spent years being shaped by God, and it shows. People don't notice that you do kind things; they realize you are a kind person. Your faith (allegiance)? No one questions you believe what you say you believe. Now, a guy at work has started asking you about it—let's just call him Guy. Doing your best to explain what you believe, admitting when you don't know something, offering prayers for him, and giving him biblical counsel, you finally get Guy interested in coming to church with you.

He gets there and is blown away. He remembers church as this dead ritual, but your church is alive and humming with the Holy Spirit. The music speaks to him, and the messages are spot on. The guy helps out at an event and then volunteers to help greet. He joins a small group or Sunday School class. After six months of listening, serving, and learning, he tells you he is ready to give his life to Jesus. He goes through whatever steps your denomination offers—sinner's prayer, confession, catechism, baptism—and is now a part of the Kingdom of Heaven.

More than that, your church (The Holy Spirit Church of What's Happening Now) is so cool that they tell him he now has a new identity in Christ, no longer bound by his sin acts or his sin nature. He is free to become a disciple(maker)!

Now what?

In many churches, the answer is a shrug of the shoulders. In others, it's an encouragement to keep doing what he's doing, which is the same as a shrug of the shoulders. This is why so many discipleship books have been written. When no one knows the path, no one sets the path. In the absence of corporate leadership, Guy gets personal leadership.

An influential person (maybe it's still you, maybe not) models for him what it means to be a disciple(maker) of Jesus. For him to fully understand what a disciple(maker) is, the mentor he chooses needs to know. I believe most churches have someone (even if it's only a pastor or elder or deacon or teacher) who can fill that role. Unfortunately, that mentor could also be a Type-A that might make him feel like he's out of his league or an Other who teaches him to demand what makes him feel good, or maybe even a Middle who models a sit-back-and-relax approach.

In other words, no path often means the wrong path.

Sadly, the wrong path is not the fault of the person leading Guy. They were led down a wrong path long ago and perpetuate what they've been taught. We learned that path from somewhere before we decided to hand it down to the next person.

As a follower of Jesus, you've been discipling someone whether you know it or not. Even if you have been completely inactive in your faith (allegiance) and it's been a long time since you repented (rethought), you have modeled that for the people around you. Most likely, your friends at church are in the same place you are. Some of them gravitated toward you because of your habits, and some of them you gravitated toward because of their habits.

We model what we learn.

This section explores how we live out being disciple (maker)s. The first section was about getting our hearts right: understanding God's plan, handling our sin acts and sin nature, and believing God is shaping us to fulfill His Purpose. Now, we are talking about loving God with our souls—our *psyche*, a Greek word for our identity, who we are, and where our decisions originate.

As people, we all come into this rite of passage with different backgrounds, experiences, and expectations. As Not Yets, we come into it recognizing our need for salvation. As Already Believers, most churches teach us that faith (allegiance) is either followed by knowledge or self-control.

HOW GOOD STUDY CAN BE BAD

Many times, the first step is to have the new believer join a class or a small group. This is a good thing, even if the church has no established path for disciple-making. After all, more knowledge helps Guy better understand what he believes. We want that, right?

He goes to class for the first time and finds out they are in the middle of Ezekiel. Habakkuk. Revelation. He wants to know more about the Bible, but he's struggling because the material is so deep. Why is it so deep? Because believers who have attended that class for years have asked to go deeper. Are they right to ask that of their leaders? Absolutely. The problem isn't the material. The problem is the baby Christian is asked to eat meat when he needs milk.

By the way, the book isn't the issue. Genesis, Romans, Matthew, any book in the Bible can be studied as milk or meat. Because of the makeup of the class, he'll need to hit the ground running to keep up. The issue is that he isn't prepared for this. The people in the class are okay with that, though. When they joined, that's what they had to do. Why should it be different for him?

Because it can lead us down the wrong path.

Have you met this person? The one that has been in the church for thirty years, almost never missing church, attending Sunday School and/or a small group for more years than they can count? Let's say for the last ten years they've heard a sermon and one lesson forty weeks out of every year. That's 800 teachings on the Bible. And yet, if you ask this person, they tell you they can't teach anything because they don't know enough? Worse, their walk with Christ hasn't changed much in the last five years. And when dissension happens in the church, they always seem to be around it.

This is one of the most frustrating things for me in my profession. What has happened? Someone convinced this person that gaining knowledge is the most important thing about discipleship. Good, right? But this is how good study can go bad for us. When we can intelligently contribute to a discussion of the conditions of Corinth in the first century, but we have been stuck in a spiritual rut for many years, we're worshiping knowledge, not Jesus. We are engaging in discipleship, not disciple-making.

At some point in years past, discipleship became synonymous with Bible study. The damage done by this hairline fracture in the truth of God has been significant. How have we tried to fix it? By teaching *more* Bible.

Don't get me wrong. I adore God's Word. It holds the words of life. But that's exactly my point. Jesus admonished the Pharisees on this exact point.

You search the Scriptures because you think that in them you have eternal life; and it is they that bear witness about Me, yet you refuse to come to Me that you may have life.
— John 5:39-40

Jesus believed so much in the Scriptures that He promised not to abolish one iota of the Law and Prophets (Matthew 5:17). He isn't teaching them to forsake their study. He reminds them of the why behind the study. Had they embraced what was taught, they would have recognized Him when He came.

This is why I don't mind having a new believer in the room when we are studying—often, Guy will remind us of the simple truths that lead us to take our knowledge out for a spin. He will wonder why, if we believe what is written, we aren't doing more of it. But that's not a good reason to drop Guy into a study without a good understanding of disciple-making already established. He could get the wrong idea about the purpose of study.

Maybe you've been taught discipleship is gaining knowledge. Don't worry, it's not too late. We are about to discover what Peter teaches about the disciple-making path. If you are willing, this teaching will prepare you even if your church has no clear path established. Yes, it's learning, too; but the purpose is not in gaining knowledge. Its purpose is to train you to live in grace, bless others, and share The Way.

THE OTHER EXTREME

Get excited to learn more about the Father, Son, and Holy Spirit. Just don't let knowledge become my object of worship. Check. Should I watch out for anything else?

Yes.

While some make knowledge their sole disciple-making process, others believe that disciple-making is a matter of behaving better. Their favorite fruit of the Spirit is self-control, but they don't really understand what biblical self-control is. Mentors who embrace this model are on a crusade to make everyone perfect(ly align to their idea of Christian ethics).

See what I did there?

Here's how it plays out. Guy is still wet from his baptism, the amen of his sinner's prayer has just left his lips, and already this person is coming alongside him to tell him of the sin he has to give up. Gladly holding Guy accountable, this person explains that his faith comes with three checklists. First, the do list:

- Attend service every Sunday.
- Be part of a Sunday School group.
- Join a midweek service or small group because by then you need the refresher.
- Wake up every morning for five minutes of Bible reading and five minutes of prayer (to start).
- Take your Bible to work so people know your life has changed. Study at lunch. And pray.
- Serve in at least one ministry, but really, the more ministries, the better.
- Memorize Scripture and quote it often in your conversations.
- You get the idea.

That list has the backing of nearly every pastor in the world, so the mentor is on solid ground. While Guy is still reeling from this daunting list, he gets the second one. The don't list changes with the denomination. I'm just going to throw some stuff out there to make you mad at me.

- Don't curse, smoke, or chew, or go with girls that do.
- Don't watch R-rated movies or television shows.
- Don't expose your kids to video games.
- Don't send your kids to public school.
- Don't enjoy adult beverages.
- Don't dance.
- Don't even use OMG when you text or talk.
- You get the idea.

This is actually a short list. Now, the things on the don't list can be spiritually rewarding choices. Pastors all over the world would be hard-pressed not to condone the list because to deny it would sound like they weren't taking a strong enough stance against sin. I wish these were the only two lists, but there's also the can't list.

- You can't be a leader in the church if you've ever had a divorce.
- You can't let anyone know you still struggle with sin because it's shameful.
- You can't serve in the church until you become a member.
- You get the idea.

This list is more insidious. Again, many pastors would say this list is meant to raise red flags, avoid the appearance of sin, help the church to remain above reproach. I'm not against any of these lists when they occupy the right place in the process (well, to be completely honest, I'm against the can't list).

I'm against making people feel like behavior modification is the same as disciple-making. We talked about this before. We tell people that salvation is by grace alone, and then we set them up to live under the law again. When our behaviors are the most important thing about us as believers, we get lost trying to police everyone. Instead of helping them learn to be like Jesus, we always end up helping them learn to be like us.

Just as knowledge cannot be our object of worship, behavior also makes a poor god. After all, if self-control worked, we wouldn't need Jesus. But we do, even after our initial salvation. When we harp on behavior, we miss the point of the freedom given to us.

Hang in there if this troubles you. I'm not talking about cheap grace, and I'm not downplaying obedience. I'm teaching how to be a disciple(maker).

If you're disturbed, then we're ready for the next step.

Come on, Middle. Keep reading, for Jesus' sake.

YOU THIS

We're a video game family. I know some believers are down on the amount of screen time kids get and the lack of physical activity that can result from playing. For us, we already build in activities that require outside. Sports leagues, hiking trips, swimming, all kinds of physical things happening in this family, so don't judge.

Video games. What we like most are the puzzles created. First-person stories where we have to make the right choices. Games where we manipulate the environment to get to the next area (my youngest son and I can play "Human Fall Flat" for hours). Adventures where we must work together to save the world or at least survive a holocaust. Our thumbs are getting great exercise, of course, but what we're really exercising is our minds.

We are all better at playing than watching. Sometimes, we forget which one of us is playing. I'm trying to navigate an environment or figure out a puzzle, and my audience is mentally right there with me. Then they see it. They know what I'm supposed to do (probably because they played it before me). I'm not even close to doing it, and I'm running out of time. They bite their lips (if it's a good day), but (if it's a bad day) they can't help blurting out the answer.

"Dad, do this!"

Which often gets the mean glare. I want to figure it out myself, but now I know the answer. Sometimes, though, I realize I never would have seen it and I'm thankful. Either way, they got my attention by the urgency they express. In effect, their tone signaled in my brain, "You're in jeopardy of missing it! Drop everything and do what I say right now!"

I'm an old guy when it comes to video games. I should be thankful. It's not that I haven't figured out how to play or that I'm too dumb to eventually get it. It's that the longer I take to figure out this part of the game, the longer I wait to get to the next cool thing. Satisfaction may come by completing it on the thousandth try, but how much time have I wasted? The urgency to accomplish the task can be lost.

In his second letter, Peter spends the salutation and his first full sentence telling us what a disciple is. He even tries to show us by how he presents himself at the beginning.

> *Simeon Peter, a servant and apostle of Jesus Christ,*
> *— 2 Peter 1:1*

He sees himself as Simeon, the servant, and by the grace of God made Peter the apostle. In the same way, we should have a sense of solidarity with other believers even if we have been given recognition or positions in the church.

Such humility allows us to recognize the divine Power of the Person who made Promises that we could Partake in His nature, fleeing from the sinful desires that formerly corrupted us and still corrupt the world. We are free and alive by the grace of God to be transformed so that others will see and ask. Disciple(maker)s live by grace as we go through our world, remembering our commitment to the One who promised to accompany us and teaching people to love God and love others. Peter finishes his description of what a disciple is and launches into an urgent message for us.

> *For this very reason, make every effort . . .*
> *— 2 Peter 1:5*

The Greek says it this way: "You, this! Move quickly on it!"

Peter knows every moment we hesitate, every moment we act like pew potatoes, and every opportunity we let pass by is a waste of time. People are hurting! They are making bad decisions! Time is running out, and they can't seem to solve the puzzle! He could wait for you to figure it out on your own, but so much might be missed. Instead of letting you rely on trial and error, he's going to solve the puzzle for you. I know that can be irritating when you're playing a game.

But this isn't a game.

If you're like me, you have a hard time seeing a movie someone tells me I must see. I can't pick up a book if someone oversells me on how much I need to read it. In everyday circumstances, I don't like being told what to do. That changes if I'm about to step into an uncovered manhole. I want you to interrupt me. I want you to alarm me, catch me up, make me pause, and change my direction. Don't tell me what to do just because you think it's right. But if you need to warn me of danger or point out a life-changing option I almost missed . . . by all means, get to the point!

Peter is saying, "You, this. Move quickly on it!"

Don't miss the urgency, and don't expect this to mean what he's pointing out will be a quick fix. Just don't wait to get started.

Started on what?

BE OUR GUEST!

If you haven't seen Disney's *Beauty and the Beast,* at least in the animated form, you either don't have any children in your family or you just can't stand Disney. I'm going out on a limb here. Even if you hate musicals, you've probably seen it.

Remember the big production number after Belle has committed to staying at the castle with the Beast? The candlestick sees her presence as an opportunity to fulfill his duty as a host and gets the whole castle to set up a dinner for her. They sing a song called "Be Our Guest!" and everyone—I mean, everyone—joins in. Furniture is dancing, plates are spinning, and all the voices in the human spectrum are harmonizing. It's loud and fun and full of energy.

It's *epichoregeo*, the Greek word translated "supplement" in the passage.

- *Epichoregeo* – the root of the word means a chorus, a production. When *epi-* is added to the front, it represents a grand production, the big number, the showstopper when all the voices harmonize and crescendo.

Peter tells us to drop everything right now and put all our effort into creating this grand production where the entire cast is harmonizing and working together. What is the cast? Faith, virtue, knowledge, self-control, steadfastness, godliness, brotherly affection, and love. In other words, Peter is anxious to get us started on creating the harmony of a life of grace.

He is describing our identity in Christ. These are the traits of a disciple(maker), but they are not stair-steps. They are added one to the other.

> *For this very reason, make every effort to supplement your faith with virtue, and virtue with knowledge, and knowledge with self-control, and self-control with steadfastness, and steadfastness with godliness, and godliness with brotherly affection, and brotherly affection with love.*
>
> *— 2 Peter 1:5-7*

THE DISCIPLE-MAKER'S WHEEL

I'm a visual person. I like to see what someone's talking about. Youtube how-to videos were made for me. If I get printed instructions, I feel like I can do it, but I always misunderstand a step. When I can watch someone do it, the parts I might miss in words become plain to me.

I want to see it to understand it.

As I studied these attributes of a disciple(maker), I realized the building was purposeful. Whatever the next step is, it not only relied on previous steps but fulfilled them. Then, a little over halfway down the list, they changed focus.

- **FAITH** is my allegiance to Jesus and lays a foundation for everything else. It's the bass in the chorus. What I believe enough to follow dictates who I am.

- **VIRTUE** is the sum of me, who I am, built on my faith lived out. It's the baritone in the chorus. Still a deep voice in me, preparing me for a life of grace.
- **KNOWLEDGE** is what I need to have faithful virtue. It's the tenor in the chorus. I can't go further until I know more.
- **SELF-CONTROL** is my will surrendered to Him. It's the countertenor of the chorus. I'm reaching new heights as I apply new wisdom.
- **STEADFASTNESS** is my loyal endurance, regardless of counterinfluence. It's the contralto of the chorus. I'm learning to persevere against myself, my world, my Enemy.

Each of these traits centers on what God is doing to me and how He is forming me to live in grace. At this point in the list, the focus changes from what God is doing in me to what I am doing with who God is making me.

- **GODLINESS** is my willingness to worship Him with all I think, feel, say, and do. It's the mezzo-soprano in the chorus. I'm learning it's really all about Him and not about me.
- **BROTHERLY AFFECTION** is living in harmony with my brothers and sisters in Christ, the Already Believers. It's the soprano in the chorus. When it's all about Him, I see His family as my family through His eyes.

- **LOVE** is godly love, unconditional love. It's the highest form, an angelic voice above and beyond the human chorus. When it's all about Him, I see the world through His eyes and can love the Not Yets just the way they are (and the Alreadys in spite of who they are).

When I look at these traits, I realize the first five prepare me to live out the last three. In the language we've been using for this series, it's the soul and mind that helps us use our strength. If I think of the change from me-focused to God-focused, I realize that's what I'm really after. Being a disciple(maker) of Jesus means being God-focused like He is.

> *So Jesus said to them, "Truly, truly, I say to you, the Son can do nothing of His own accord, but only what He sees the Father doing. For whatever the Father does, that the Son does likewise."*
>
> *— John 5:19*

Like I said, I'm a visual person. I worked with my friend Natalie Newlin, and we came up with this diagram. We call it The Disciple-Maker's Wheel.

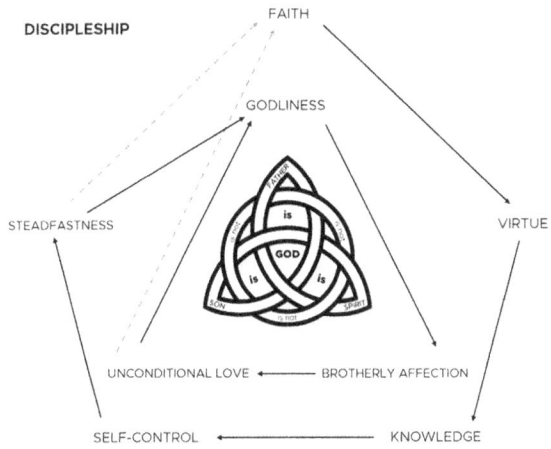

When I am grounded in faith, I become a different person who wants to know more about how to live for God regardless of the circumstances. As I focus on Him, I am led to love the church and the world. The outer wheel leads to the inner wheel, where we are closest to God.

Ever go to a conference, or hear a specific message, or take a mission trip and find yourself suddenly on a spiritual high? Maybe it happened when you were first saved. Maybe it hasn't happened since and you've been wondering why. I believe we experience this spiritual high when we are living out the inner wheel.

If you've felt that high, then you know it doesn't last forever. Over time, it wanes. What do we do about it? Beat ourselves up? Question the experience? Bite our lips and try harder? I've tried all these, and none of them worked. Instead, as the diagram shows, we should realize we are being driven back to faith. Returning to faith is not the same as starting all over. We have a new normal, a reset because our faith is greater than it was. We are given the opportunity to rediscover the truths we've learned and build on them!

Unfortunately, much of our discipleship in the last century has been built on a little different model. We've had a tendency to make one of two mistakes that have left us Middles out of the equation. I know we just talked about this, but the wheel helps us visualize it.

Faith to Knowledge

The mistakes have to do with our treatment of the new believer. Our efforts to lead someone to Christ revolve around grace. We want them to know they haven't done enough to earn Heaven on their own, and they never will. We want them to know they've done enough to condemn themselves, and they can never repay the debt they owe. Then, we introduce them to the grace of Christ and tell them they haven't done enough wrong that Jesus can't forgive them. We tell them they no longer need to be perfect to try to get to heaven.

> *For our sake He (God) made Him (Jesus) to be sin Who knew no sin, so that in Him (Jesus) we might become the righteousness of God.*
> *— 2 Corinthians 5:21 (parentheses mine)*

Then, when they become Christians, we bombard them with one of two priorities that are important, necessary, but out of order. The first thing we try to do is move them from faith to knowledge.

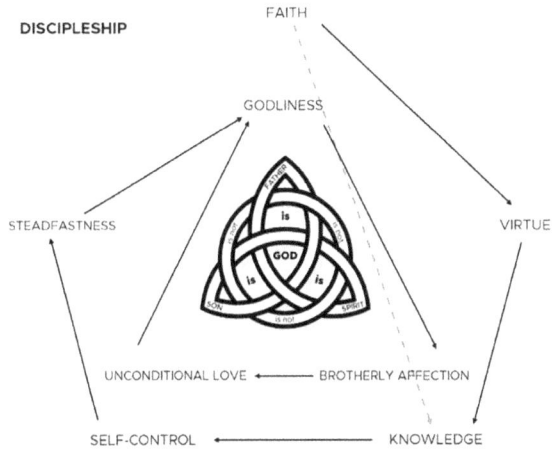

Study and memorization of Scripture are integral to the faith, right? Very important! I believe this, as well. The problem is that too often, we accidentally create this equation in the minds of the new believers:

DISCIPLESHIP = KNOWLEDGE

As important as knowledge is, this is just not true. When we act as though it is, we put the new believer in jeopardy. He will read his Bible and go to a class and listen to sermons and think he is growing. She will be able to answer biblical questions and win Bible trivia games, but she will wonder why she isn't experiencing the abundant life.

The other issue is when we take our new, grace-filled believers and introduce them to the new rules of life.

Faith to self-control

Our new believer comes fresh into the faith and is accosted by a new set of rules even more difficult to follow than the old rule. Jesus wants us to be holier even than the most religious people of His day, so we begin immediately to train the baby Christian in what they can and cannot do to stay a part of the faithful. If we aren't careful, we may accidentally teach them that they now need to be perfect to remain qualified for heaven.

> *Therefore, whoever relaxes one of the least of these commandments and teaches others to do the same will be called least in the Kingdom of Heaven, but whoever does them and teaches them will be called great in the Kingdom of Heaven. For I tell you, unless your righteousness exceeds that of the scribes and Pharisees, you will never enter the kingdom of heaven.*
>
> *— Matthew 5:19-20*

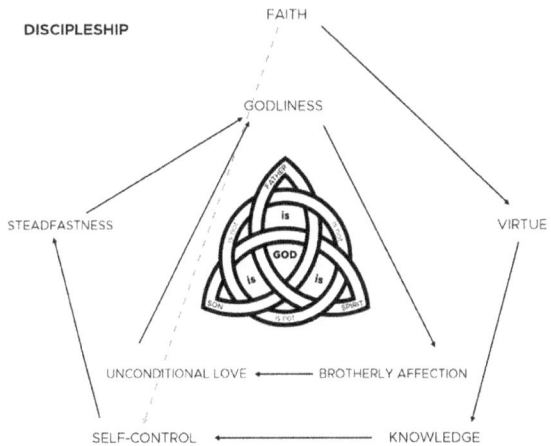

Obedience is important, right? Integral to the faith, something that is repeatedly commanded in Scripture. The problem is too often, we create this equation in the mind of the new believer:

DISCIPLESHIP = OBEDIENCE

Sounds biblical and true, doesn't it? But it's not. If discipleship were all about obedience, we'd all be in trouble. Notice that passage in Matthew just quoted, Jesus drops some hints that this isn't true. He doesn't say those who relax one of the commandments are lost. He says they are the least. He doesn't say those who do them are the only ones who qualify. He says they are great. Then, He hints at His salvation offer. The only "righteousness that exceeds the scribes and the Pharisees" is the one we receive when we put our faith in (give allegiance to) Jesus.

We can't "self-control" our way into heaven, and we can't "self-control" our way to keep our place in heaven. We can only throw ourselves at the merciful feet of Jesus.

> *For by grace, you have been saved through faith. And this is not your own doing; it is the gift of God, not a result of works, so that no one may boast.*
>
> — *Ephesians 2:9*

Peter teaches a better way.

I don't want us to get ahead of ourselves, but it's important to understand why these two shortcuts don't work. Faith in knowledge can lead us to think we just need to have the right answers to get God's approval. Faith in self-control makes us think we just need to behave a certain way to get God's approval.

We need grace to get God's approval.

Grace has an inherent advantage over the other two options: by nature, it changes our nature. We become less focused on ourselves for our sake and more focused on God for His sake. We are changed without relying on our own efforts to change us. We are set free, released from the bondage of shame because when we fall short and are guilty, grace covers us. We don't study less; we study more. We don't obey less; we obey more. Grace motivates us because it no longer needs to be for us. We are doing it for our family, our loved ones, our friends, our acquaintances, and the strangers we meet (and even for our enemies).

We don't need it for us—Jesus saw to that—but people need it from us. Middle, you aren't being asked to do a spiritual self-improvement routine. You are being asked to prepare yourself so that as you go through your world, the people who love you, need you, and meet you are introduced to Jesus, who can save them, too.

You're part of a movement. You're a rebel of contentment. You're an adventurer in your daily routine. You're an ambassador in your hometown. You're a Middle placed in the middle on Purpose for the glory of God.

You are a Grace Agent.

Peter gives us a battle plan for every day, and it begins where every good song begins: with the bass line.

DADDY SANG BASS

God believes in you.

When you were born, He decided not to make you a robot. He didn't predetermine all your decisions. He didn't exercise His sovereign right to put you under His thumb. He's more secure than that in Himself. He knows what bad bosses don't know: your decisions do not determine His worth as the Master. He gave you the right to choose your own path. He gave you free will to elect to accept His love or not. The world didn't begin with you. The struggle between God and evil didn't begin with you. You didn't begin with you. He is the beginning.

I am the Alpha and the Omega, the first and the last, the beginning and the end.

— *Revelation 22:13*

This is the beginning of faith (allegiance).

The bass line of all God intended you to be is simply your response to His faithfulness. Do you recognize Him as the Creator of the Universe? Do you recognize His sovereign right to determine our moral code? Do you recognize your guilt before His code? Do you accept the willing sacrifice He made on your behalf? Do you believe He wants to transform you into the best you can be for the sake of those around you?

This is the content of faith: to give your allegiance to the Person with the Promises.

Knowing Who He is and what He Promises should cause us to rethink (repent of) the lives we lived before we knew Him. Once we've found the One we can trust, our next step is to give our allegiance to (put our faith in) Him. Jesus, Man of Sorrows, Who died and rose again to relieve us of the penalty for our sins, fill us with His Holy Spirit, and Promise us eternal life, deserves our full devotion. These blessings are the beginning of our faith (allegiance), not the end.

We trust God for our salvation and now must trust Him to help us live as new creations. Saying, "I trust God," but never putting Him to the test is like saying, "I trust spaghetti

174

is good," but never eating any of it. We don't really trust until we've given someone a chance to prove trustworthy. We can't just say we believe in God. We must give Him our allegiance.

This is what Paul calls "the obedience of faith" (Romans 1:5).

Our Father in Heaven trusts us to make our own decision to believe His Son died to save us from our sins. We decide to stake our whole lives on the belief that He will grant us the Power to follow Him and extend eternity to us. From this point on, we will trust His way of living and expect the reward of kept Promises.

The main Promises are the Spirit and eternal life. The second one, we won't know until we get there if we were right to put our trust in God. The first one is the guarantee that proves His trustworthiness for the second. The Spirit, working in us, is our pledge. When we see Him working in our lives, that kept Promise gives us confidence in the Promise of Heaven.

> *For this reason I bow my knees before the Father, from whom every family in heaven and on earth is named, that according to the riches of His glory He may grant you to be strengthened with power through His Spirit in your inner being, so that Christ may dwell in your hearts through faith . . .*
>
> *— Ephesians 3:14-17*

Daddy sang bass, then promised if we begin by singing along with Him, He will help us with everything else.

175

BUILDING YOURS

Some truths about faith:

- **Faith is about God and not us.** A Gentile woman is asking for healing, but Jesus tells His disciples He was sent only to Israel. She won't stop crying to Him, so He tells her it isn't right to give the children's bread to dogs. She doesn't argue with Him or tell him He has no right to treat her that way. She recognizes her faith is in what God will do, not who she is. "Yes, Lord, yet even the dogs eat the crumbs that fall from the Master's table." Jesus is overcome by her faith (unusual in His ministry) because she spoke of God's mercy, not her value. (Matthew 15:21-28)

- **Faith is not about how much belief we have.** Jesus comes down from the Transfiguration to find the disciples arguing with a man whose son is possessed by a demon. The disciples can't heal the boy, but the man won't give up. "If you can do anything, have compassion on us and help us." Jesus is taken aback. "'If you can!' All things are possible for one who believes." The man responds in the correct way. "I believe; help my unbelief!" He realizes in that moment it isn't the amount of belief, but the Person he puts his faith in. (Mark 9:14-24)

- **Faith doesn't happen after results but before them.** An official asks Jesus to heal his son. Jesus tells him,

"Go; your son will live." The man believes Him and returns home. He is met by servants who tell him his son was healed at the same time Jesus spoke (which is the same moment the man chose to believe). We can't wait for results to believe in God's blessing. We give our allegiance first, then we see the results of our faith (John 4:45-54).

- **Faith is in a Person, not in the Word, although the Word is the Person.** Jesus is admonishing the Jews for refusing to believe in Him. He tells them they delve deeply into the Scripture, seeking eternal life, yet they refuse to believe in Him. Notice He does not condemn their deep study; He condemns their unwillingness to see Him in their study (John 5:39-47). They do not see the Word in the Word (John 1:1).
- **Faith changes how we see people.** Jesus is teaching forgiveness and the disciples are overcome by the hardship His teaching creates. They tell Him, "Increase our faith!" They know they will need to give allegiance to Him to do what He is asking. After Jesus tells them it isn't about their amount of faith, He says a servant isn't applauded for doing his service. He is expected to do his service. If they have any faith at all, they should be able to see people as opportunities for grace, not objects of condemnation. (Luke 17:1-10)

I don't know about you, but this faith thing has always seemed difficult to me. How do I believe what I can't see? How can I prove what won't be proven until I die, and even then, only to me? How can I know if I'm right?

Jesus blows all that out of the water. It's not about us, or how much we believe, or what results we get, or how many verses we can quote, or if we're up to it. Our faith (allegiance) is completely, solely, truly dependent on Him. He is the One Who has to prove trustworthy, not us.

Now, are you ready for me to blow your mind? Maybe you won't respond the same way I did, but I hope what I share next will help you understand what this teaching means for you.

OUR FAITH IS EQUAL

Let's go back to the beginning of that second letter of Peter. We're going to look at his salutation again, remember what we've learned, and then see the earth-shattering truth he places in the middle of it.

> *Simeon Peter, a servant and apostle of Jesus Christ, to those who have obtained a faith of equal standing with ours by the righteousness of our God and Savior Jesus Christ:*
>
> — *2 Peter 1:1*

Did you catch it? It's easy to miss. He is Simeon Peter, not just Peter, to remind us of his life before Jesus. He is a servant before an apostle to remind us his position does not place him above us but puts him in service to us. Then he drops the bombshell.

Our faith has an equal standing with Peter. Equal. With Simeon Peter.

You remember Simeon Peter? The guy whose boat was filled with fish on a night when they caught nothing? He's the first one to recognize the holiness of Jesus and fall to his face to say, "Depart from me, for I am a sinful man, O Lord" (Luke 5:8).

Simeon Peter who was the one to answer when Jesus asked the disciples who they said He was. The same guy who said out loud for the first time, "You are the Christ, the Son of the living God" (Matthew 16:16).

Peter, one of the twelve chosen by Jesus, was given the keys to the Kingdom of Heaven.

Peter, one of His inner circle, who experienced the Transfiguration and Gethsemane.

Peter, who received the Holy Spirit in the upper room and preached the very first sermon.

That Peter. Walked on water. Healed the beggar at the Beautiful Gate.

Your faith (allegiance) is of equal standing with his.

How is this possible? Only by the righteousness of our God and Savior, Jesus Christ. Our faith (allegiance) is not equal to his because of how great we are. It's Who we trust, not how much we trust, that makes us equal. Our faith is not less than his because of how great his deeds are. It's Who he trusted, not how much he did, that makes us equal.

> *To those who have obtained a faith of equal standing with ours BY THE RIGHTEOUSNESS OF OUR GOD AND SAVIOR JESUS CHRIST…*
> — *2 Peter 1:1b (emphasis mine)*

The Person with the Power to make the Promise that we may Partake in His nature sees our faith in Him as equal to that of Peter's. This is the bass in our chorus. We aren't in a faith test, and we aren't in a faith contest. God isn't working to increase our faith because He is disappointed in us but because deeper faith will make us more effective.

Faith (allegiance) is the beginning, the foundation, but our faith (allegiance) is made powerful because of Him. Stop trying to think of ways to increase your faith. Simply have enough faith (give your allegiance) to take the next step.

It only takes a mustard seed.

THE BARITONE: VIRTUE

Right before Thanksgiving, when I was in the first grade, our teacher had us trace our left hand on a plain white sheet of paper. She then had us draw little stick legs on the bottom of the palm and something she called a "wattle" under the tip of the thumb. Then we drew a little pilgrim hat on top of the thumb and realized suddenly that we had drawn Tom Turkey. She then gave us colored pencils so we could bring Tom to life. By the time I was done, I could no longer see the handprint. I only saw my turkey friend.

The following year, my new teacher tried the same thing, but she wanted to save some time. She took a black marker, traced her own left hand on a plain white sheet of paper, and made copies. After handing out the copies, she had us do the exact same steps to make Tom Turkey. Saved her lots of time, but I was left unsatisfied. My second-grade brain couldn't help but see the handprint. No matter how much I used the colored pencils, Tom would not come to life.

What does this have to do with disciple-making? Everything.

Rather than start with teaching us what to know or how to behave, our first addition to Daddy's bass line is who we are. Not who we were; that wouldn't be very helpful. Since Jesus saved us and the Spirit filled us, we are not the same anymore.

Therefore, if anyone is in Christ, he is a new creation. The old has passed away; behold, the new has come.
— *2 Corinthians 5:17*

I love this passage because it reminds me the old Michael died with Christ, and the new Michael rose again to live for the first time (also see Romans 6:4). We're going to come back to it later to realize the context, but for now let's bask in the brilliance of God's remaking of us. Our new character, our new identity, is in Jesus.

This is where Peter leads us after we have offered our faith (allegiance) in Him. Not new knowledge, not better behavior: new *being*. You might even say, new *psyche*. Remember from the first two volumes that this is the Greek word used in the Great Commandment when Jesus says we should love God with all our souls.

> *For this very reason, make every effort to supplement your faith with virtue…*
>
> — *2 Peter 1:5a*

- **Virtue** – *arete* in the Greek, which describes the sum of our qualities, our traits. Some English versions translate this word as "moral excellence."

Listen, Middle. Those who have tried to reach you by helping you understand the effort you need to put into your new sense of faith (allegiance) were not wrong about that. Their mistake was thinking.

1. The effort was in learning or behaving
2. The effort was entirely yours.

This will be a theme over the last pages of this book and one we need to understand if we are going to be serious about being disciple(maker)s. Every "effort" we make is a Partnership, not a personal accomplishment. God will *always* be the controlling interest in that Partnership, but we will have to be willing participants for His Purpose to be effective.

When we understand it completely, it will be like my first-grade Tom Turkey. I give God my handprint, and He gives me the directions and the colored pencils to become the me He created me to be. If we try to go from faith (allegiance) to self-control, our behavior modification may be successful, but it will be like someone else creating a handprint for us and letting us draw Tom Turkey. The handprint that is part of the picture won't be us, it will be them—and we will never fully get rid of the impression that we are being shaped by someone other than God.

We are involved in the transformation God is causing in us, but He will not be satisfied to let us be transformed into someone else's idea of who we are. That's not even the difficult part. This is also true: we are also involved in the transformation of those we disciple, but we must resist the temptation to try to make people follow Jesus the way we follow Him. We have to let God use *their* handprint and His colored pencils *their* way.

Regardless of the current spiritual status of the one we disciple—Not Yet or Already—we will find it necessary to convince them that God is the Senior Partner and they are the Junior. To do that, though, we will have to believe it ourselves.

What does it look like for God to direct our new identity? We will have to trust Him to transform us. Does that sound strange? It shouldn't. My hope is that it will help you understand a particularly troubling passage in Philippians. Maybe you've run across it before and wondered what it meant.

> *Therefore, my beloved, as you have always obeyed, so now,*
> *not only as in my presence but much more in my absence,*
> *work out your own salvation with fear and trembling . . .*
> — *Philippians 2:12*

Paul is speaking here to a well-known group of believers who have been learning from him how to follow Christ (remember what we learned about 2 Timothy 3?). This isn't about obeying every law of God but about remembering how to walk in the Spirit as Paul has instructed. Then he says his presence shouldn't change their effort.

If they truly wanted to walk in the Spirit, they would have to work it out themselves. The words translated here as "fear and trembling" have roots in *phobos,* where we get phobia, and *tromos,* which means to shake. Literally, it means to shake with heightened fear as you process what your salvation means for you.

Man, that sounds like the Truth-Only Gospel, doesn't it? Behavior is the ultimate goal here, and even though we are saved, we should be scared to death as we try to hold onto it. But that's only half the sentence. What's the rest say?

> *. . . for it is God who works in you, both to will and to*
> *work for His good pleasure.*
> — *Philippians 2:13*

This passage comes directly after Paul's great passage about the humility of Christ and how He bowed to the Father by becoming a man and suffering death on the cross. His humility should humble us! Paul tells us that the presence of leadership shouldn't have to prompt us to live the way Jesus lived. Instead, we should, in our own humility that comes out of our character (*arete*), realize what a God-sized order this is. Good thing, then, that God is the One working it in you!

He is transforming you. You are not transforming yourself. How? By grace. If we relied on the Truth-Only Gospel, the Law would have to transform us. If we relied on the Grace-Only Gospel, we wouldn't have to worry about transforming. But Paul wants us to see how the Grace and Truth Gospel tells us the Spirit is working on that part from the very beginning.

> *For all who rely on works of the law are under a curse; for it is written, 'Cursed be everyone who does not abide by all things written in the Book of the Law, and do them.' Now it is evident that no one is justified before God by the law, for 'The righteous shall live by faith.'*
>
> *Galatians 3:10-11*

The Galatians are being reprimanded because they fell prey to those who wanted them to believe they had to become Jews first before they could become Christians. He gets so upset that he calls them foolish and under a spell (Galatians 3:1). He wants them to know the Law isn't the way anymore. Walking by faith in the Spirit of grace is.

> *But the law is not of faith, rather, 'The one who does them shall live by them.' Christ redeemed us from the curse of the*

law by becoming a curse for us—for it is written, 'Cursed is everyone who is hanged on a tree'—so that in Christ Jesus the blessing of Abraham might come to the Gentiles, so that we might receive the promised Spirit through faith.
— Galatians 3:12-14

Once again, God is in the redemption business. He redeems our past, present, and future when He frees us from the Law and places us under grace. Our response is to allow Him to transform us so that our will becomes His will so that His works are our works. Instead of learning to behave better, He transforms us into someone who *is* better. We just have to use His colored pencils to dress ourselves like I once did Tom Turkey. What are those colors?

Put on, then, as God's chosen ones, holy and beloved, compassionate hearts, kindness, humility, meekness, and patience, bearing with one another and, if one has a complaint against another, forgiving each other; as the Lord has forgiven you, so you also must forgive.
— Colossians 3:12-13

AH, THERE'S THE RUB

Mmhmm. Got to talk about forgiveness again. It's the one thing that frees us up so that God can transform us. Let's walk with Jesus a little and be His disciple so we can become His disciple-maker.

Jesus is dropping truth bombs right and left when He talks about how angry God gets when someone causes another to sin. He tells them to watch themselves and then tells them how to watch out for their fellow disciples.

> *"Pay attention to yourselves! If your brother sins, rebuke him, and if he repents, forgive him, and if he sins against you seven times in the day, and turns to you seven times, saying, 'I repent,' you must forgive him."*
>
> *— Luke 17:3-4*

His followers are so blown away by this that they ask Him to increase their faith! Acknowledging how hard it is, Jesus tells them even the faith of a mustard seed can uproot trees, which is a way to say they should already have enough faith (allegiance) to do this.

Later, slick Peter tries to show off. Jesus is teaching how to handle it if a brother sins against us. We leave our gift to God at the altar (it's that important!) and go to lovingly confront him. If he won't listen, we bring another to confirm what we've seen in him. If that doesn't work, we're to bring him before the church and ask him to repent. The whole point of the passage is not discipline but redemption. Then Peter shows off that he's been listening to his Rabbi:

Then Peter came up and said to him, "Lord, how often will my brother sin against me and I forgive him? As many as seven times?"

— Matthew 18:21

I bet Peter was proud of himself at that moment. Where the first response had been a request to increase their faith, this time he's jumping in and offering to do what Jesus taught—to forgive his brother seven times. Except, Jesus' lesson wasn't about the number. His lesson was about forgiveness.

Jesus said to him, "I do not say to you seven times, but seventy-seven times."

— Matthew 18:22

Some versions quote Jesus saying, "Seventy times seven," but we Bible nerds who argue about it are missing the same point Peter did. Whether 70 or 490, the number is not the lesson.

Forgiveness is the lesson.

Here's what I'm learning about how God transforms character: The faster His grace becomes our grace, the faster we transform. When we can forgive people the way Jesus forgives us, we open the door in our souls to *be* a certain kind of person, predisposed to all those great things listed as the fruit of the Spirit. That's why Jesus often connects His forgiveness of us with our forgiveness of others.

Where can we find that? Right in the Sermon on the Mount!

> *"For if you forgive others their trespasses, your heavenly Father will also forgive you, but if you do not forgive others their trespasses, neither will your Father forgive your trespasses."*
>
> — *Matthew 6:14-15*

Jesus isn't warning us about losing our salvation. That transaction hasn't happened yet. This is pre-cross, pre-resurrection. This is about recognizing that when we forgive, we partake in (*koinonos)* the nature of God; so when Already Believers forgive, they show the character (*arete*) of God to the people around them.

If you aren't willing to forgive, how much do you really understand? If God's grace is not your grace, do you comprehend God's grace? For further study, look at the parable of the unforgiving servant found in Matthew 18:23-35. Notice the proximity to the previous verses.

Our willingness to see ourselves from God's perspective, repent of (rethink) our former way of life, put our faith in (give allegiance to) Jesus, and let Him transform us causes us to see others from God's perspective, too. We are no longer the Behavior Police in a Truth-Only Gospel. We are the disciple(maker)s of Christ, full of grace and truth.

Through forgiveness, the sum of our qualities, our virtue, is redeemed by God to reach the souls (*psyches*) of other people.

We are suddenly more loving, filled with more joy, people of peace, infinitely more patient, kinder than ever, good to all we meet, faithful to God, gentle to those who disagree with us, and better able to control our temptation to sin and our responses to others. This aggregation of our traits begins to express the fruit of the Spirit.

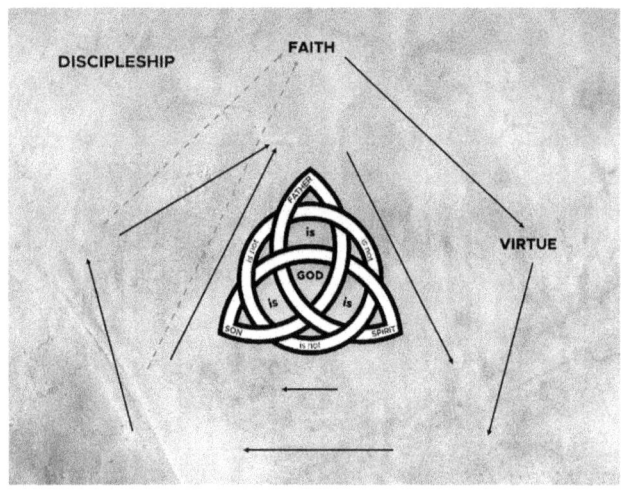

MIND:
Knowledge, Self-control, Endurance

My prayer is that many of you have been traveling with me from the beginning. This road that started in *Rethink* finds purpose in *Follow* and leads us to the truths in this volume. In case you are new to the journey, however, I want to take a moment to explain the structure we are using.

From the Sermon on the Mount, we derive from Jesus a pattern that we follow by dividing each book into three parts: Know, Be, Live. In discovering what we need to know, we start with the tension that we are trying to solve—with the heart of the matter. This is the same as what we just discussed about virtue. We do not start with new teaching. We start with where our hearts are.

Once we understand the tension, we can then learn new knowledge to find a path forward in our faith journey. We ask ourselves what God wants us to be and whether we are willing to believe this new revelation and become more like His Son, Jesus. This second part confronts what our souls need to be transformed.

The third part helps us know how to live out who we are to be after learning this new knowledge. We separate this part into the different aspects of our nature addressed by Jesus in the Great Commandment to love God with all our hearts, souls, minds, and strength.

Our hearts are where our treasure is—will it be tuned to the Kingdom of Heaven or the kingdom of me?

Our souls are in dire need of salvation—will we accept that our decision-making is rooted in sinful selfishness and seek help from Jesus?

Our minds naturally conform to this world—will we be transformed as God renews us?

Our strength—our resources, from bodies to finances to societal position—is not enough by itself—will we call on the resurrection power of the Holy Spirit?

So far, we have discovered in Peter's letter that we have the same faith (allegiance) he has because we trust the same Person, and that Person is interested in winning our hearts. His Purpose is to fulfill His Promise that we may Partake of His divine nature and He has the Power to bring about that result. Our hearts can be His because He is trustworthy. Therefore, He begins working on our souls—our identity, the root of who we are, and what causes us to make decisions—so that our identity is in Him and not coming from ourselves or from the world.

We must turn now to the mind.

TRUE KNOWLEDGE

My wife helps me pastor The Jar and selflessly does so without pay. Her "day job" is a social worker at a hospice company in town. When a new client is added to their roster, she visits with them and their family and helps them navigate all of the forms and benefits required by government agencies, transitional care facilities, and funeral homes. That's the bones of her occupation, but the meat is the spiritual, emotional, and mental support she gives. She is as called to that as any pastor is to a pulpit ministry.

Part of her responsibilities is to find volunteers who will help with some of the office work and provide special support, like making sensory quilts for those with dementia. They also give their time to sit with clients, sometimes to allow caregivers a chance to run errands but often just to provide companionship as a part of the client's quality of life wellbeing.

I gladly serve as one of her volunteers. When she discovers a man who needs company, she sends me to spend an hour a week just asking questions and listening. Sometimes, I get to pray with those men, but often, I just get to hear their stories. The longest I've maintained a relationship with a client is now running three months (which proves that hospice is not only for the last days of a person's life).

Over those three months, I have listened to him tell me stories about his school days in elementary, secondary, and college grades. I know where he went, what towns he called home, and what work he did. I know the woman he loved for over fifty years before she passed away. I know his sister and have spent some of my time talking to her. I've heard his son's voice on the phone.

I know him.

But I don't know him the way his sister does or how his wife did. There's an intimacy there I can't match. We talk an hour a week—they've spent a lifetime with him. I hear the same stories sometimes and catch new details—they lived the stories with him. I know (*gnosis*) him, but they really, really, really know (*epignosis*) him.

When Peter has established that faith (allegiance) is the bass line and virtue (the sum of our traits, our character) is the baritone, he moves on to introduce us to the tenor of our *epichoregeo,* our big show number.

> *For this very reason, make every effort to supplement your*
> *faith with virtue, and virtue with knowledge . . .*
> — *2 Peter 1:5*

Bible nerds are starting to celebrate. We finally get to the meat! But hold on, my fellow wordsmiths. The first step on this part of the journey is to understand what kind of knowledge Peter means.

The Greek word *gnosis* denotes knowledge in general. Our liberal arts education in America is meant to give us a well-rounded view of the world. When my youngest daughter went to college, she decided not to declare a major yet. Before she decided what she wanted to choose as her focus, she wanted to wander around in the general knowledge of things to decide what most interested her. What she sought was *gnosis*.

Once she acknowledged her love of writing and discovered the deep connection she had with history, she declared her intent to get a degree in both History and Creative Writing. Those two majors became her whole world. Math would help a little, but became less important. Science became restricted to the kind that promoted her understanding of history or the crafting of a sentence. Taking a biology class could help some, but taking an archaeology class would align more clearly with her interests. What she now sought was *epignosis*—a clear, distinct topic that she wanted to understand thoroughly.

Peter wants us to get to the center of our faith. The prefix *epi* denotes that perfect center. Not just the bullseye on a dart board but the point in the center of the bullseye. To get to that defined center of a subject, *epignosis* is to know it better than you know anything else. Over and over, Peter uses this version of "knowledge" in the letter.

> *His divine power has granted to us all things that pertain*
> *to life and godliness, through the knowledge (epignosis)*
> *of Him who called us to His own glory and excellence…*
> — *2 Peter 1:3 (parenthesis mine)*

For if these qualities are yours and are increasing, they keep you from being ineffective or unfruitful in the knowledge (epignosis) of our Lord Jesus Christ.

— *2 Peter 1:8 (parenthesis mine)*

For if, after they have escaped the defilements of the world through the knowledge (epignosis) of our Lord and Savior Jesus Christ . . .

— *2 Peter 2:20a*

The basic doctrine of Christianity is so important that we can't have a true understanding of faith (allegiance) without it. To believe the Gospel requires that we understand the Power behind the Word of God and the tenets proposed there. That's the *gnosis* of our relationship with God.

Jesus is the *epignosis*. To fully give our hearts, souls, minds, and unified strength in love to God, we must make Jesus the focus of our study. We can know the Bible, but James says the devil and his fellow fallen angels know that (James 2:19). As I mentioned earlier, the Pharisees knew the Torah, the Histories, the Prophets, and the Writings better than anyone but Jesus told them they missed the whole point (John 5:39-40). They had *gnosis* but missed the *epignosis*.

We can know about Jesus the way I know about my wife's client, but Peter wants us to know Jesus like that man's wife or sister did. Deeply, intimately, personally. Not just His history but His heart, soul, mind, and strength.

GRACE AND PEACE

If you've been paying attention, you know that through our study so far of 2 Peter 1:1-8, we've missed a whole verse. Just as we went back to pick up verse one, it is time to go back and visit verse two. In this passage, Peter also uses *epignosis*, and I believe it holds a key to the kind of personal knowledge of Jesus our author wants us to have.

> *May grace and peace be multiplied to you in the knowledge of God and of Jesus our Lord.*
>
> — *2 Peter 1:2*

Not only is this more defined version of knowledge used here, but Peter wants that knowledge to do something to us. If we have delved into this kind of understanding, two things are multiplied in us. That word, multiplied, is *plethuno* in the Greek, and it means to be maxed out, to be filled to maximum capacity. If *epignosis* is the next step in the *epichoregeo* of our relationship with God, and if the purpose of that kind of knowledge is to focus on Jesus and become like Him, then what is maxed out in that knowledge tells us much about the qualities of that Person.

Peter gives us the answer at the beginning of the sentence.

- **Grace.** The Greek word *charis* can mean grace, gift, favor, or blessing.
- **Peace.** The Greek word *eirene* can be translated peace, but it can mean more than a lack of conflict, as in

197

peace from war. Often, it means a lack of internal conflict, a peace of mind, a wholeness connected to an understanding of ourselves.

So, the two big takeaways at the center of the knowledge of Jesus have to do with living in the favor and blessing of God and being free of internal conflict because of our wholeness as persons. Out of these qualities, we are able to make decisions that align with the will of God because we are acting out of the character of the Son of God. We know Jesus is a man of grace. He is blessed and lives in the favor of His Father.

And behold, a voice from heaven said, "This is My beloved Son, with Whom I am pleased."

— Matthew 3:17

[Jesus] was still speaking when, behold, a bright cloud overshadowed them, and a voice from the cloud said, "This is My beloved Son, with Whom I am well pleased; listen to Him."

— Matthew 17:5 (brackets mine)

I've always loved that God honored the baptism of Jesus by speaking to the people there and telling them before He had a chance to accomplish much that He was pleased with His Boy. Even better, after Jesus is preparing to finish the work, God doesn't just say He is pleased with His Son; He is *well pleased* with Him. The first encouragement helps Jesus get started, and the second encouragement is greater because it helps Jesus finish strong.

God's favor followed Jesus to the cross, to the tomb, to the resurrection, and to the ascension. God's favor is on Jesus now and will be still when He returns for us. Because of the grace of the cross and tomb, we get to experience the favor of the resurrection and ascension with Jesus one day.

Peter prays for us that the favor and blessing, the grace and the gift, are maxed out in our hearts.

Which, more than anything we can get from inside ourselves or from the world, gives us an internal peace that can't be measured. For fun, read through the four Gospels of Jesus Christ and count how often Jesus tells someone to "Go in peace." He doesn't mean, "Go and don't start any trouble." His invitation is for them to keep the freedom from the internal conflict He solved for them by healing their hearts, souls, minds, and bodies.

When Jesus sends His disciples out to preach and heal, He tells them to look for worthy houses where they can stay. If they find no worthy houses, they are to leave those places and take their peace with them. He's not counseling them to leave without causing trouble. He wants them to leave without any internal conflict.

On the way to Gethsemane, Jesus gives some last instructions. In the middle of those important lessons, He warns them that trouble is coming. Then, He gives them the key to being faithful through those troubles.

"I have said these things to you, that in Me you may have peace. In the world you will have tribulation. But take heart; I have overcome the world.

— John 16:33

Despite all they will go through—arrests, mockery, beatings, death—Jesus tells them they can meet those challenges without internal conflict because Jesus went through them all before they did, and He overcame all of it through His resurrection.

Speaking of that, when Jesus pops in on the boys after the resurrection, His first words to them are, "Peace to you!" (Luke 24:36). They are still frightened, though, so He meets them in their doubt with His reality. At the end of the day, this is what it means to have this kind of peace. To look at our circumstances and say, "But God . . ."

We can meet any challenge and have peace if we remember the reality of Jesus.

Rejoice in the Lord always; again I will say, rejoice. Let your reasonableness be known to everyone. The Lord is at hand; do not be anxious about anything, but in everything by prayer and supplication with thanksgiving let your requests be made known to God. And the peace of God, which surpasses all understanding, will guard your hearts and your minds in Christ Jesus.

— Philippians 4:4-7

I hope this passage means more to you now than it ever did. We can rejoice—have joy and confidence regardless of circumstances—because Jesus is right with us. Why would we be anxious? That internal conflict isn't necessary! Instead, when we start to feel anxious, we can go to God in prayer and thank Him for being with us to the end of the age. The result is a resolve, a new level of trust, that whatever happens, we need not be roiled in internal conflict.

Our hearts and our minds are guarded by Him.

Which is worth our exploration here. The heart mentioned in this passage has already been addressed by our repentance (rethinking) and our faith (allegiance). Our souls—our identity—have been addressed by our faith (allegiance) and our virtue (who we are). This "mind" that is guarded helps us understand how knowing Jesus gives us peace.

The Greek word for mind in this passage is *noema*, which specifically denotes the final output of our thinking. The conclusion of our mental process. In other words, the way we come to an understanding of what our decision should be.

In the favor, blessing, and grace (*charis*) we get from Jesus, we can now act from the lack of internal conflict (*eirene*) He gives us to make decisions that align with God's will. We are armed with the right perspective to do what God wants in any situation.

We act from the intimate, personal, deep knowledge (*epignosis*) of the One Who saved us, redeemed us, and transformed us into new creations.

We know Jesus . . .

. . . so as to walk in a manner worthy of the Lord, fully pleasing to Him, bearing fruit in every good work and increasing in the knowledge (epignosis) of God.
— *Colossians 1:10, parentheses mine*

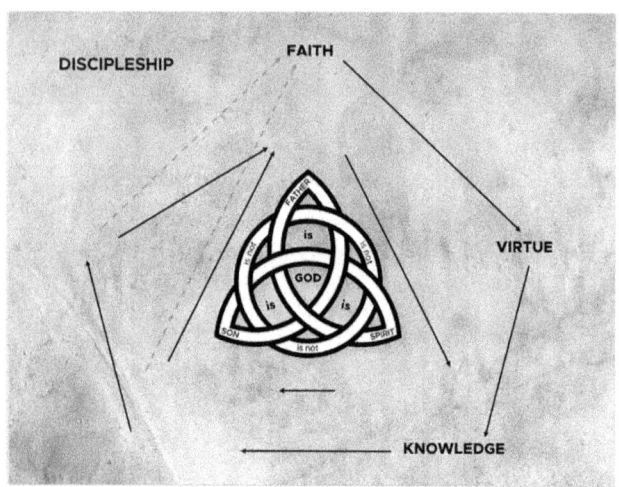

HOLDING OUR WATER

As our faith deepens (bass), our character rises toward excellence (baritone). The more our character resembles Jesus, the more we hunger and thirst for knowledge about the kind of righteousness He offers (tenor). If this sounds self-centered still, in a way it is. Self-centered, though, not self*fish*. To be selfish is to operate out of a desire to please ourselves. What we are doing is letting God improve us for the sake of others: we are being filled to be emptied. The outer wheel prepares us by filling us with His Spirit and the foundation He offers so that the fruit of His Spirit empties out on those around us.

This is important to understand as we go into the next step of building our harmonic chorus (*epichoregeo)* in disciple-making by adding the countertenor.

> *For this very reason, make every effort to supplement your faith with virtue, and virtue with knowledge, and knowledge with self-control…*
>
> 2 Peter 1:5-6a

Remember, we are still talking about loving God with all our minds. But that's where the toughest battle seems to take place. So many influences in our culture today are keeping us from hearing the voice of God. We feel assaulted on every side as we try to build ourselves into the kind of man or woman He has made us to be. We can feel disheartened in our efforts to become like Jesus. No wonder we're buying into the lie, the stronghold, that says the church can't be saved.

We have a hard time believing we can be saved ourselves!

Well, we don't put it in those words. But when we think of the corruption that is in the world (that rotten tomato) and what we are called to be (Partners Partaking in the Promises), we see more tomato than we do Jesus sometimes.

I have to be honest; I struggled with this step being a part of the disciple-making process. It seems to go against everything Peter says in the first five verses. God is the One Who gave us the Promises, the Power, the opportunity to Partake. His grace and peace are supposed to help us become what we can't be by ourselves.

And then He asks us to have self-control? Isn't that just another divine bait-and-switch?

When I looked into the original language, I was shocked by the mental image the Greeks conveyed when they considered self-control. *Egkatreia* means to have mastery over oneself, but it can also be used to mean continence. In a phrase that isn't used often in English anymore, it calls to mind the idea of "holding your water."

Like you really, really, really have to relieve yourself, and you are nowhere near a bathroom.

Forgive me for the crass language, but it's necessary for us to get the concept. Think about a time you had to pee and you weren't in the right place, in the right circumstances, or at the right time to do it. You were in line as a bridesmaid at your sister's wedding. You were in fifth period at school and had forgotten to go during lunch. You were in the last fifteen minutes of the movie at the theater, and that large soda was barking.

This is what it means to have self-control. And here's the thing: no one can hold your pee for you. In fact, no one would be upset at you for how you're feeling. They wouldn't blink an eye if you went to relieve yourself in an appropriate manner.

You are only offensive if you choose to relieve yourself in the wrong place, in the wrong circumstances, or at the wrong time.

Isn't this a great way to describe how we feel when temptation comes our way? Often, what we are feeling isn't the issue—how we relieve the feeling is the real issue. Let's just consider some positive things that could be Promises that become rotten tomatoes.

- **SEX.** God made sex, so it isn't sinful in and of itself. Although sex isn't love (we get these confused), He did create sex to be enjoyed within the confines of marriage as He defines it. But if we choose to engage in sex in the wrong place, in the wrong circumstances, or at the wrong time...

- **FINANCIAL SUCCESS**. I can't believe we struggle with this, but we do. God wants us to prosper and doesn't mind us being wealthy—some of the women who followed Jesus were wealthy enough to fund His ministry. But if we get our earnings from illicit dealings, or we use them only in a selfish manner, or if we sacrifice our family to get it...

- **SELF-CARE**. I know I struggle with this. When do I need to serve my self-interest, and how do I avoid becoming selfish? I want to be like Jesus, but I know He didn't neglect His own heart, soul, mind, and body. Where self-interest operates with a sense of the right place, circumstance, and time, selfishness operates in spite of the wrong place, circumstance, and time.

- **FRUSTRATION.** You knew this would make the list, right? Frustration is a red light on our dashboard that can tell us something is not right. It can also cause us to act in ways that are not right—even when it feels right. If you go to the bathroom but pee in the sink, you're still not operating in self-control.

These are meant to be representatives that relate to all of us, but the list goes on and on. God intended that we enjoy this life, but not at the expense (or offense) of others. If we aren't careful, we can feel like we are following God but relieving ourselves all over ourselves and others.

Hey, I did apologize for the crass language.

God expresses three influences on us that will cause us to become incontinent (there, is that better?). Most of us immediately think of the devil making us do it. Yes, that is one. But I think the enemy is many times quite willing to kick up his heels on his desk as the other two influences do their work. The first is our own selfishness. Paul often calls it "the flesh."

For the desires of the flesh are against the Spirit, and the desires of the Spirit are against the flesh, for these are opposed to each other, to keep you from doing the things you want to do.

— *Galatians 5:17*

The rebellion that started in the Garden when Eve decided the fruit looked tasty no matter what God said is still occurring in our hearts today. That nature still fights us despite God's willingness to forgive it and give us all we need to live godly lives. We want what we want when we want it, and self-control in this arena means delaying our own personal gratification until we can understand what our *pneuma* is saying to our *psyche*.

Remember those from the first two books? In case you missed it or don't remember, we will only revisit the New Testament reference for review.

Now may the God of peace Himself sanctify you completely, and may your whole spirit (pneuma), and soul (psyche), and body be kept blameless at the coming of our Lord Jesus Christ.
                    — 1 Thessalonians 5:23 (parentheses mine)

The word translated spirit can mean wind, breath, or spirit. The word translated soul is used to describe our identity, who we are, and what dictates how we make our decisions. The first Greek word, *pneuma,* is the only one used of the Holy Spirit. Think of it this way: God has made you in His image and given you His ability to understand the place, the circumstances, and the timing. As we listen to His Holy Spirit, our own spirits begin to understand what God would have us do. Yet we have an opportunity in our *psyche*, our souls, to make up our own minds about what we will do.

Cartoons illustrate this with the proverbial angel and devil on our shoulders, but that's too simple. This isn't just divine intervention (although the Spirit gives that). This is who we are designed to be warring with who we are right now—the divine accesses the Power to Partake in the Promises, but not unless we are willing to let our identity be in the Person Who made those Promises. Will we listen to the flesh or the Spirit? Are we going to hold our water or just let it all out?

The second influence is actually a corporate version of the first. Where we individually make mistakes, miss the mark (what the Bible calls sin), we also collaborate with others to make that sin seem okay. The more people are doing it, the more "normal" it feels. This is another way to say *culture*, but not all culture is bad. Only when we become so accustomed to missing the mark that we make it the mark do we find culture has a bad influence on others.

> *Do not love the world or the things in the world. If any-*
> *one loves the world, the love of the Father is not in him.*
> *For all that is in the world—the desires of the flesh and*
> *the desires of the eyes and pride of life—is not from the*
> *Father but is from the world.*
>
> *— 1 John 2:15-16*

Notice the word flesh in John's description of the world. In other words, the desires that reduce us to less than divine, the ones that look so pleasing to the eye, the ones that build up pride and self-governance rather than humility and walking in the Spirit, these collective "norms" cannot change what God has said is true. We can't say, "Well, everybody's doing it."

That's not a moral compass—that's being tossed about on the winds of change.

> *If any of you lacks wisdom, let him ask God, who gives generously to all without reproach, and it will be given him. But let him ask in faith, with no doubting, for the one who doubts is like a wave of the sea that is driven by the wind.*
>
> *— James 1:5-6*

We will talk more about this in a later volume when we discuss our frustration with the world. For now, learn this lesson. When our *psyche* wants to do what everybody else is doing, we have the right and the privilege to ask God to direct us. But we can't ask and then wonder if God is right. Once we hear what God has to say, we must be willing to accept His wisdom over the world's. When we do, we will be forced to act as a counter-revolutionary among the people in our circle of influence.

How does the enemy figure into this? He pushes on our bladder.

Let's get one thing straight. The devil is not the antithesis of God. he is not ever-present like God, he is not all-powerful like God, and he is not all-knowing like God. he and his minions (notice I *never* capitalize when I speak of him) do have an influence on this world, though. All he really has is deception and accusation. Corruption is ours, and destruction comes through us when we listen to his lies and his attempts to make us feel shame.

So, I want to take that power we have given the devil away from him. The devil didn't make us do it. The devil gave us an alternate perspective on our lives, and we chose to listen to him and do it ourselves.

When we do, we pee all over ourselves.

Sorry. Crass again.

Self-control, then, is rightly named but not rightly understood. We don't show it through behavior modification. We show it through submission. When we are willing to believe that God is right 100% of the time, we will operate in self-control. What must occur in us to accomplish that?

First, we hear the bass line. We must be willing to give our full allegiance to Jesus.

Then we hear the baritone. We let our character rise to meet the character of Christ.

Then we hear the tenor. We study to understand who God is and who we're meant to be.

Have you ever heard someone practice singing harmony to a song that is playing in their earbuds? When the melody is absent, it sounds discordant. Wrong. We wouldn't choose to listen to it by itself. But when that same person sings harmony with the rest of the praise team at church, we feel the completeness of it, how it fills out what is already there.

Self-control is not your faith, but it harmonizes with it. Don't sing it by itself.

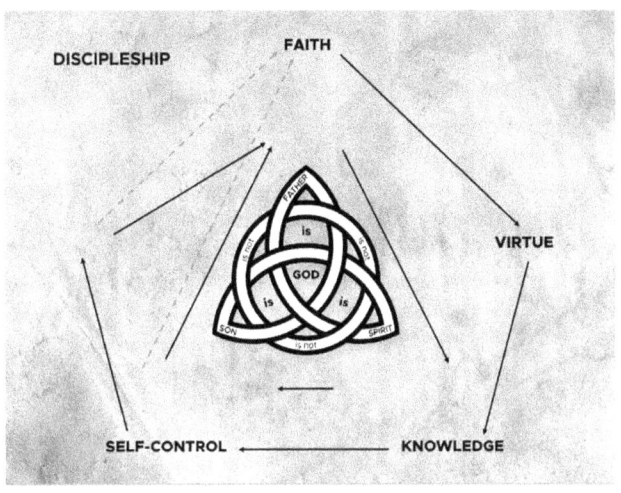

WHAT I WISH HE HAD LEFT OUT

You can imagine—maybe you've experienced it—what the world thinks about us adhering to a bunch of old writings about what is right and what is wrong. When culture decides something is now okay, those who contest the will of the majority are called unenlightened, judgmental, phobic.

They might say, "That's how the world *used* to think, but we have progressed and moved forward. We know *better* now. What was once considered missing the mark is now a new expression of our wisdom, our new knowledge, and our understanding of how the world works. To hang on to that old way of thinking is to refuse to progress. Why are you scared to let this new thing be true?"

As I said, we'll talk more about this in a later volume, but we can't ignore the result of this truth right now. Because it is directly related to Peter's next trait of a disciple(maker).

For this very reason, make every effort to supplement your faith with virtue, and virtue with knowledge, and knowledge with self-control, and self-control with stead-fastness . . .

2 Peter 1:5-6

Here is the last step in being filled by God so that we can be emptied for others. The bass line is our faith, the foundation of everything. The baritone is virtue—not what we know or how we behave—that is becoming ever more like Jesus. The tenor is knowledge, but not knowledge about Him; knowledge *of* Him. The countertenor is self-control, which is more like humbling ourselves to live God's way than choosing the right things ourselves.

The contralto, then, is steadfastness. The root word in Greek is *hupomone* and is best translated as "to remain under." To be steadfast is to remain under the control of God even when it's hard. Some of the hardest English words can be used to express it. Endurance. Perseverance. Longsuffering. It's the courageous part of living for Jesus, more courageous than our first allegiance to (faith in) Him and why it's so hard to maintain that faith in (allegiance to) Him.

This is more than being patient, more than just keeping our own personal integrity. This is not doing the right things, no matter what others think. This is living to give Jesus the glory in everything we do even when (not if) we are persecuted for it.

> *Only let your manner of life be worthy of the Gospel of Christ . . . standing firm in one Spirit, with one mind striving side by side for the faith of the Gospel, and not frightened by your opponents.*
>
> — *Philippians 1:27-28a*

Paul wrote this just before he took a whole chapter to tell us about the humility of Christ. I don't think this is a coincidence. For us to live for Christ, we must be willing to suffer whatever others think about us, say to us, or work against us. That takes a kind of patient endurance that goes beyond what most of us are willing to do for our personal integrity.

Honestly, this last piece of the outer wheel that defines disciple(maker)s is the one that causes the others to crumble most. This is the world's influence on us. They are willing to hate us rather than see the falseness in themselves.

When I wrote that last sentence, I almost changed it because I envisioned how others would feel when they read it. The temptation was to make it less offensive by giving them the benefit of the doubt. But I can't give them the benefit of the doubt if I really love them. They need to know that God's truth is Truth so I can tell them about the heart of His Truth, grace. If we aren't willing to call missing the mark what it is—sin—we will never get them to understand why they need a Savior. So, I *must* live a godly life that glorifies Christ if I want to reach them with His love. Sometimes, they hate me for it because...

> *This is a clear sign to them of their destruction, but of your salvation, and that from God. For it has been granted to you that for the sake of Christ you should not only believe in Him but also suffer for His sake, engaged in the same conflict that you saw I had and now hear that I still have.*
> — *Philippians 1:28b-30*

I used to think Paul was saying that our willingness to suffer persecution to do God's will was a poke in the eye of the people who are going to be destroyed by Him. Doesn't it sound like that? It's their destruction, but it's your salvation! Show them how good you are so they can really feel bad about themselves, and even if they don't, you're saved, and they are not!

But I don't think so anymore. I think Paul is trying to drive home that the difference between us and them is not our behavior but God's grace. We once were shown the clear sign of our destruction. That's why we reached out for Him. When we did, God gave us our salvation.

Listen. We aren't becoming godly to show they are not, and we aren't godly to shame them for who they are. We are godly to show them they, too, can be transformed. *Steadfastness isn't for us!* I believe this is why we are on the cusp of a transition. Though steadfastness is a mind frame where we choose to glorify Jesus with our lives no matter what, it ultimately has a greater influence on those around us than it does on us. That's why Jesus loves the persecuted so much!

> *"Blessed are you when others revile you and persecute you and utter all kinds of evil against you falsely on my account. Rejoice and be glad, for your reward is great in heaven, for so they persecuted the prophets who were before you."*
>
> — *Matthew 5:11-12*

Your reward in heaven isn't great because you sustained your integrity. It's great because you showed those who watched that your allegiance to (faith in) Jesus wasn't a fad, and it wasn't just a choice among many—it is the key to eternal life!

Did you catch that? The person persecuting you may not be the one influenced by your willingness to repent (rethink) and exhibit your faithfulness (allegiance) as a disciple(maker). Others are watching how you handle yourself and deciding if this Jesus is worth following. If you fold like a wet napkin, they will decide He is not. If you withstand the persecution, they just might decide He is worth exploring.

Think of what Jesus said. We are to rejoice and be glad because our reward will be like the prophets of old. What did the prophets do? They foretold doom and gloom to the kingdoms of Israel and Judah at the direction of God. They waited, they prayed, and they acted under God's authority to warn the people to return to Him.

Who listened?

Very few in the audience, evidently, because exile still occurred. Yet they also hinted that grace would be offered, that a Messiah was coming, that salvation was at hand, and that the Kingdom of God is greater than any kingdom on earth. Who listened to that? A handful of Jews who saw their Rabbi rise from the grave and bring the Kingdom of God to Jews and Gentiles alike.

Those who are affected by the outcome of our persecution and the steadfastness of our faith (allegiance) will have to rethink (repent) what is important and choose whether or not to become a disciple(maker) of this same Messiah. But what about the ones who are doing the persecuting?

> *"You have heard that it was said, 'You shall love your neighbor and hate your enemy.' But I say to you, 'Love your enemies and pray for those that persecute you, so that you may be sons of your Father Who is in Heaven.'"*
> — *Matthew 5:43-44*

Just like God, we must be willing to see these "enemies" of ours as the lost children the Father is seeking. They are the one sheep for whom God would leave the ninety-nine. They are the lost coin that matters more than all the found ones. They are the ones the angels rejoice over if they are willing to come home (see Luke 15).

First of all, then, I urge that supplications, prayers, intercessions, and thanksgivings be made for all people . . . This is good, and it is pleasing in the sight of God our Savior, who desires all people to be saved and to come to the knowledge of the truth.

— *1 Timothy 2:1, 3-4*

Yeah, but what about all the people in authority? What about the ones who make all the laws, or change our church's stance on biblical doctrine, or who threaten us with sanctions and criminal proceedings? Do I have to pray about them?

Did you notice I left a verse out of that Timothy passage?

...for kings and all who are in high positions, that we may lead a peaceful and quiet life, godly and dignified in every way.

— *1 Timothy 2:2*

God sees the enemy differently than we do. We think we are struggling against people. God knows our struggle is on a spiritual level, and the people who do these things are captives, not combatants. The point of seeing them this way? That we would lead godly lives that glorify Jesus. Why? So others can be saved because God wants to save them all.

Steadfastness is the first step to emptying ourselves for the world.

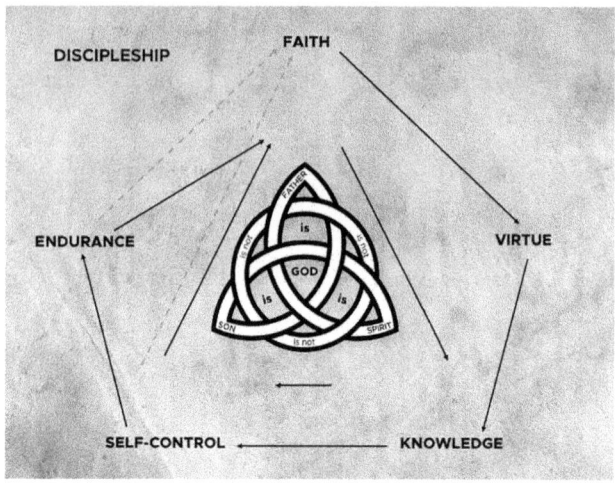

I'm sorry, guys (some of you gals, too), but I have to point this out. As we build this *epichoregeo*, we find that the first wheel is about becoming focused, which appeals to our masculine hearts. We want to learn what it means to be soldiers in God's army. But when we get stuck in the military frame of mind, we can justify some pretty ungodly ways of treating people.

Steadfastness is the first female voice in the choir, and it speaks to treating relationships with people with a new level of importance. We pray for those who persecute us, pray for those who see us persecuted, and praise God for the opportunity to suffer for Him (look at the response of the disciples to persecution in Acts 4). Yes, we are the army of God. But our greatest weapons are faith, hope, and love.

Don't worry, shieldmen and shieldmaidens, these weapons are the strongest in the world. We aren't displaying weakness but meekness that can overcome the world.

"I have said these things to you, that in Me you may have peace. In the world you will have tribulation. But take heart; I have overcome the world."

— John 16:33

STRENGTH:
Godliness, Brotherly Love, Agape

We're getting ready to land the plane, so to speak, but it's important to remember how we got here. This series is about the real frustrations we feel as faithful followers of Jesus Christ as we consider the current state of the Church. In *Rethink*, we admitted we can't start with others; we must start with ourselves. In *Follow*, we explored what the Gospel is and how it not only strengthens our faith but sharpens our focus on what it means to trust the Good News of Jesus. In this book, we have been exploring what it means to fulfill the mission of the Gospel: to make disciple(maker)s.

But when we try, we find ourselves operating out of a stronghold of the enemy when we believe nothing can be done to save the "Big C" Church. Admitting that, we agreed to focus on the 70% in the middle of our churches (I count myself one;

do you?) who aren't discipling self-starters but are willing to be disciple(maker)s if someone will explain why they should make the effort and convince them that they are capable of it.

Our focus text has been 2 Peter 1:1-8, which uses the concept of an overarching, massive chorus number where the melody and harmonies bring about the pure song of heaven…

- BASS – Faith (allegiance), the foundation for all else.
- BARITONE – Virtue (not knowledge or self-control), who we are and not what we do.
- TENOR – Knowledge, the kind of personal knowledge only friends can have.
- COUNTERTENOR – Self-Control, which is misleading. It's letting God have control, not taking control of ourselves.
- CONTRALTO – Steadfastness, endurance, persistent obedience regardless of reward or consequence.

Now we are ready for the last three voices, and they blend like any good aria ever sung in an opera. Two of them are human.

But God…

IMAGINE YOU ARE A JAR

Every day, your role is to be filled with water so that water can be used on other things. Over time, people pick you up and pour out your water to refresh someone, to bring life to plants, to cleanse things, to entertain children. As they use you, what happens? It depletes and gets lower and lower. And the people? Sometimes they have accidents, don't realize what they are doing, or even purposely misuse you and cause chips and cracks in you. Now, you are being depleted from use and from abuse.

You're a jar. You can't fix the cracks, can't replace the chips. No matter how broken you get, you can't fix yourself. Without help from the owner, you will never be more effective than you are right now.

You're a jar. You can't fill yourself back up. No matter how low the level of water inside you gets, you can't take yourself back to the well. Without help from the owner, you will never be more full than you are right now.

But God is your Owner. Where people have used you and abused you, God is the One Who cares for you, lovingly fills in the chips, mends the cracks. He *is* the well, the source, the reason you have water at all. His water is living water, His purpose is to fill you to empty you, His great pleasure is to keep you safe and mend you when another mishandles you.

Keep this illustration in mind as you think about what we've learned. Though we've explored what it means to be filled, we must remember the Owner does the filling. He prompts us to faith. He changes our character and virtue. He gives us the knowledge. Submission to Him is real self-control. And when it's tough, He is the One Who helps us endure.

Because this is true, we must be aware of the trap of thinking that now it's up to us. Just as the filling is done by the Owner, the emptying is done by Him as well. The emptying comes in waves, and it follows a familiar path. The Living Water of the Holy Spirit pours out of us to love God, love the church, love the lost.

We think too often that it's our grace, our gift, to love that way. But we don't have the capacity. We need the gift of God to be the people of God.

> *Jesus answered her, "If you knew the gift of God, and who it is that is saying to you, 'Give me a drink,' you would have asked Him, and He would have given you living water."*
> — *John 4:10*

As we learn to be emptied, let's also learn to be honest with ourselves.

For too long, we have been trying to fill ourselves and empty ourselves. Or, sometimes better and sometimes worse, we have been waiting for some other person to fill us or empty us. We've tried it all; doing it on our own, following a pastor, following a teacher, following a mentor, following a leader. Every time, we do everything humanly possible to be a better Christian.

But God . . .

Let's try a new perspective. Let's let Him do it. We *need* to be filled, and we *get* to be emptied, but God is the only Owner Who can do it. Oh, goodness; when we get ahold of this, we will suddenly be a fountain of eternal life for everyone on the planet.

> *Jesus said to her, "Everyone who drinks of this water will be thirsty again (every one who tries to fill their lives from*

*a human perspective will never have enough, be enough,
do enough), but whoever drinks of the water I will give
him (does it My way with My power under My direction) will become in him a spring of water welling up to
eternal life."*

— *John 4:13-14 (parentheses mine)*

As we pool our resources to be disciple(maker)s, watch how
Peter's list swells into the higher voices so that we can almost
hear the angelic chorus awaiting us when Jesus takes us home.

SEE HEAVEN

I believe the one whom Jesus loved (we know this is John) wrote
his Gospel with two things in mind: the divine love of Christ
and the divine perspective we can have because of it. It can be
summed up in the mystical truth that Jesus is fully God and
fully man, allowing Him to live as the kind of man the Father
intended to live on this earth. We'll talk more about this later.

When Jesus knew He was not much longer for this earth
(between the Last Supper and the Garden of Gethsemane),
John records that He gave a last teaching and prayer. During it,
he tells His disciple(maker)s the secret to living the same kind
of life.

*"I am the true vine, and my Father is the vinedresser. Ev-
ery branch in me that does not bear fruit He takes away,*

225

and every branch that does bear fruit He prunes, that it may bear more fruit."

— John 15:1-2

We could teach deeply just on this passage, but let's take what's on the surface for now. Jesus is telling us three things:

1. He is the source of life for them, the vine that gives them nourishment.
2. His Father, however, tends them and expects them to produce fruit.
3. Both the one bearing fruit and the one not bearing fruit will experience discomfort, the latter to their destruction, the former for greater production.

If we read this from the perspective of a Grace-Only Gospel, this passage doesn't make sense. How can God expect something from us if grace relieves us of any expectation? If we read this from the perspective of the Truth-Only Gospel, we might misunderstand this passage to mean we can never be good enough or produce enough fruit. We need a Grace-and-Truth perspective to understand it and to remember that Jesus wasn't done teaching yet.

"Already you are clean because of the word that I have spoken to you."

— John 15:3

This forces us to give up the Truth-Only Gospel perspective. Jesus isn't saying they are obligated to produce fruit, or they will be destroyed. They are clean because they have listened to His Word and have believed in Him and on Him: each disciple(maker) has decided what Jesus says is true and, therefore, has decided to believe Jesus is the Messiah and worth following. Already, they are worthy because of their faith (allegiance).

Truth-only Gospel believers are squirming right now. But wait. Jesus isn't done.

"Abide in me, and I in you. As the branch cannot bear fruit by itself, unless it abides in the vine, neither can you, unless you abide in me. I am the vine; you are the branches."

— John 15:4-5

See what He does? He gives a Grace-Truth in the beginning with a warning that the Father, the vinedresser, is going to use his shears on us, prune us, and make us more fruitful through discomfort. While He does this, some who do not bear fruit are going to be exposed as being separated from the vine, Jesus, and will wither and die on their own. He cuts them off because they are now a threat to the rest of the plant.

Then Jesus gives us Grace to remind us that we are clean because of Him, not because of our efforts. Our faith in His Word and His person are enough to position us in Him. We can rely on this as the foundation for our life following Him.

227

Finally, Jesus gives us Truth to remind us that being connected to Him means following Him and following Him means producing fruit. If you truly believe in Him, He cleans you. If you truly believe in Him, fruit comes out of you. He finishes up where He started, reminding us that we don't have the ability to provide the nourishment it takes to produce fruit.

I call this the divine perspective of Jesus. He sees us through the lens of Grace and Truth, and each in equal measure. That's what it means to see Heaven. The concept hides in a definition of an English word we don't use very often anymore: Abide.

An old definition of abide is to live in something. Like I can say, "I abide in my apartment, house, RV, etc." But we don't abide in them; we reside in them. To abide is something more.

A newer definition of abide is to accept something. Like I can say, "I abide by your decision." This can almost feel like we are begrudgingly giving approval because we can't change it anyway. To abide is something more.

A last definition of abide is to tolerate something, and it is often used in the negative. "One thing I can't abide is a person who talks too much." The positive version of that points again to giving begrudging approval to something that we are asked to accept.

The Greek word in this passage is *meno*, and it means to wait, to await, to remain, to stay. It almost has a sense of lurking under the surface, anxiously awaiting the opportunity to make itself known. Here, Jesus uses it in the context of being the vine that gives us life. It's His life that gives us life and leads us to eternal life. If we abide in Him, He is always lurking under our surface, threatening to come out in us and show life.

When we abide in Him, we show Him to the world. Know what that does? Yes, it produces fruit. That means we must be constantly aware of our relationship with Him. We don't pray to check off a list—we pray to abide. We don't read the Bible to prove we're Christian—we read to abide. We don't gather with the church to meet an obligation—we gather to abide.

To allow Him to lurk beneath our surface, watching and waiting for opportunities to show the world the love He has for them through us. That means we must see Heaven to be heavenly to bring Heaven here (notice, another version of Know, Be, Live). Peter's next entry on the list speaks to that.

> *For this very reason, make every effort to supplement your faith with virtue, and your virtue with knowledge, and your knowledge with self-control, and self-control with steadfastness, and steadfastness with godliness...*
>
> *- 2 Peter 1:5-6*

The next voice in the choir of Heaven is the middle female voice, the mezzo-soprano. Like the viola in an orchestra, sometimes unnoticed between the cello and the violin, this voice rarely has its own solo but brings the other two voices together. Not just a filler, the mezzo-soprano (and the viola) *completes* them.

In the same way, godliness completes the connection between being filled by God and being emptied by God. The

Greek word is *eusebio* and means to act in a pious way, to be holy, to worship God with our lives. We might think of it as complete devotion to God in Heaven, so much that we are devoted to the cause of Heaven.

What is the cause of Heaven? The Gospel! Remember how we defined it in book two, *Follow*?

> *Good News! The Kingdom of Heaven is reclaiming earth through the life, death, and resurrection of Jesus Christ of Nazareth, God's only Son. We who repent of our sins and give allegiance to Him are forgiven and empowered by the Holy Spirit to spread His influence as we boldly follow in His footsteps.*

This requires a heavenly perspective, just as Jesus had. John records a number of conversations where the Messiah is trying to elevate the eyesight of the person in front of Him. Sometimes, it's by healing physical blindness, but often, it is about relieving someone of spiritual blindness.

Nicodemus wants to find eternal life, but Jesus wants him to be born again.

The woman at the well wants water, but Jesus wants to give her the Living Water.

The disciples want to feed Jesus at the same well, but Jesus' food is to do God's will.

The disciples can't feed the five thousand, but Jesus knows the Father will.

The people want Jesus to be their baker, but Jesus gives them the Bread of Life.

His brothers want Him to reach for fame, but Jesus reaches for truth.

The Pharisees want Him to condemn the adulterous woman, but Jesus extends grace.

We could go on, but by now you see the pattern. Often, what humans *want* is not what Jesus gives. He has a higher perspective, and His desire is to help them see what they really *need*. By ourselves, we can't maintain this perspective. It's almost like we are branches of a vine, and if we try to do it on our own, this kind of awareness just dies off. But if we are connected to the vine, this kind of awareness lurks beneath the surface as we remain in Him long enough to let Him change our perspective for us.

This is godliness. To be so in tune with Jesus that we see things from His perspective and worship Him by living out what He would do to fill their needs and not their wants. To see the least of us the way He sees us and act accordingly.

How can we do that? By starting with the bass line and letting God fill us to prepare us for emptying. Our faith will lead to a change in our virtue, causing us to seek knowledge that allows us to submit our self-control to Him so that we can endure the pruning it takes to produce our awareness of His will. Just as faith is the foundation for the outer wheel, godliness is the foundation for the inner wheel.

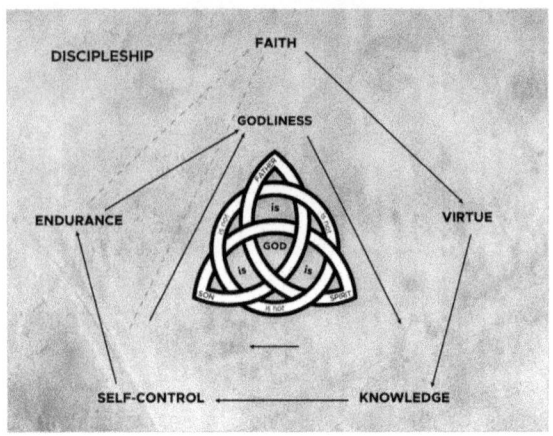

BE HEAVENLY

If, despite coming to the end of the third book in this series, you are still frustrated and mad at the church, this is going to be difficult for you. Once again, God confronts us with our sin of bashing and complaining about His Bride. I'm struggling, too, but I can't deny what Peter wrote nor what Jesus said.

> *For this very reason, make every effort to supplement your faith with virtue, and your virtue with knowledge, and your knowledge with self-control, and your self-control with steadfastness, and your steadfastness with godliness, and your godliness with brotherly affection...*
> — *2 Peter 1:5-7a*

"A new commandment I give to you, that you love one another: just as I have loved you, you also are to love one another. By this all people will know that you are my disciples, if you have love for one another."

— John 13:34-35

See it? In Peter's passage, he doesn't just say to love all people. He says to supplement our devotion to the Father and the cause of Heaven with an affection for our brothers and sisters in the faith. This echoes the "new commandment" Jesus gave His disciples. How is it new? He has been teaching them how to love the world despite its inconsistency, selfishness, and cruelty. Now, He tells them what will truly separate them from everyone else.

To love each other.

He must have known. It's hard to love the members in a church. Sometimes, we aren't sure they *are* members of the Church. Of course, God doesn't equivocate for us and tell us it's okay to stop loving people even if they aren't members. In fact, He's about to tell us our job is to love everyone unconditionally anyway.

But that doesn't come first. No, we need practice to get there. We need to build a community to provide for them before we do that. So Peter tells us that this part of the chorus, the soprano, the highest human voice attainable, is to love our brothers and sisters with the affection we reserve for very close family and people who are not related but we count as family.

Paul even uses a combination word for love to express it in Romans.

Love one another with brotherly affection. Outdo one another in showing honor.
— *Romans 12:10*

In this passage, "brotherly affection" is the same word Peter uses in our chorus of voices. But the word he uses to start the sentence is *philostorge*, a combination that sheds light on what Peter is teaching here.

C. S. Lewis did a treatise on how the Greeks used four different words for love that made their way into the Bible and called it *The Four Loves*. I encourage you to read it if you haven't already. What follows is my understanding, not a take on what Lewis wrote. He's just better than me at explaining it, and I wanted you to have that resource.

The three loves that are humanly possible in Greek, in the order of their depth, are:

- *Storge* – a family love. It's how you talk about that one relative that always seems to cause problems. "I know he's trouble, but he's family, and I have to love him."
- *Eros* – a romantic love. It's the warm bubblies you get when that certain person is near and the desire to share intimacy (not just physically) with them. Read the Song of Solomon.

- *Philos* – a brotherly love. It's the people in your life, family or not, that you know you can count on and who know they can count on you. A great example in the Bible is David and Jonathan.

We will talk about the fourth love in the next section. For now, though, notice what Paul did when he references the love we should have for other members of the church. He combined the basest human love and the highest human love into one word, *philostorge*. That means when we approach our brothers and sisters in Christ, we *have* to love them because they are family, but we *learn* to love them like the brothers and sisters they are. How important is that to Jesus? Look at the last sentence of the passage I quoted earlier.

"By this all people will know that you are my disciples, if you have love for one another."
— *John 13:35*

That's why this is a new commandment. We have to start here. We have to love our brothers and sisters in Christ the way Jesus loves them. If they are going astray, we lovingly reconcile them. If they are living for Jesus, we lovingly encourage them. If they are serving Jesus selflessly, we lovingly join them. If they are serving themselves selfishly, we lovingly come alongside them and show them a better way.

Philos is the soprano, the highest human love, and it is sometimes not enough when we are dealing with humans, so

Paul gives us a combination that helps us understand this isn't about condoning or permitting other believers' sins. It's about loving them as that family member who causes trouble and then learning to love them as brothers and sisters as they grow.

When we commit to that, our gatherings will be heavenly. But we can only do that if we can see Heaven. Now, we're ready for divine love…

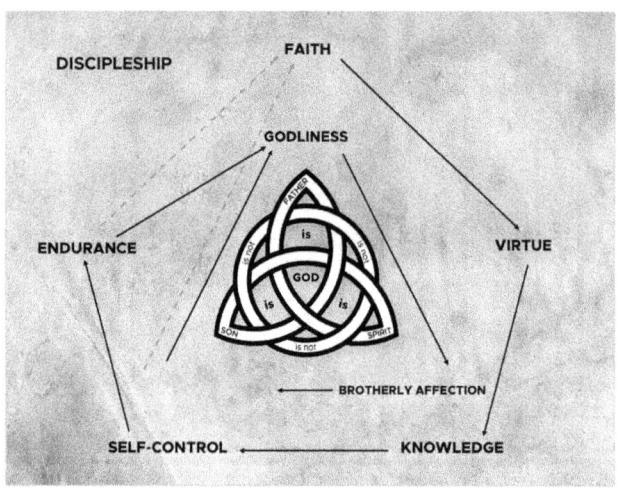

BRING HEAVEN HERE

Carrie and I hadn't been married long, and we typically had too much month at the end of our money. I was in banking, and she was working for a shoe store, but we learned something about marriage that we didn't know: after the wedding your income doubles, but your bills are squared. I don't know how that works, but it does. I took an evening job serving tables at a Denny's restaurant to help us pay down some of those extra expenses.

One night, a couple came into the restaurant. I sized them up (as servers often do) and tried to find a unique way to welcome them. They were young and obviously in love. She was positively glowing. I surreptitiously glanced down and saw the telltale baby bump. I jokingly grabbed two adult menus and a children's version and said with a big smile, "Table for two and a half?"

Her face fell. His face glowered. I quickly put the children's menu down and led them to their table. Walking back to get their drinks, I saw my two fellow servers hiding behind the soda fountain with their hands over their mouths and glee in their eyes. Begging them to take the table did no good. They wanted to see how I was going to handle it when I went back.

I didn't want to go back. What was I thinking? A guy should never go up to a girl and assume by her appearance that she's pregnant! I got two glasses, filled them up, and set them on the tray. During a busy evening, I could do that in about fifteen seconds. That night, it took five minutes. I just couldn't work up the nerve.

Eventually, I headed to the table. Even from a distance, I could see she was crying. Crying! Never mind the tip; as a fairly new believer, I couldn't forgive myself for hurting someone like that. I carefully approached them and saw that they were holding hands. As I set the drinks down, I blubbered about how sorry I was for what I said.

She started shaking her head, and I saw joy in her eyes as she said, "No, you don't understand. I *am* pregnant. I just hadn't told him yet!"

We all had a good laugh at my expense as I took orders from this young married couple embarking on a new season of life. I learned something that day. It's still not okay to assume a woman is pregnant, but it is possible for God to fix your stupid!

One of my preacher friends reminds me of that all the time. We can be spiritually discerning and socially awkward at the same time. God doesn't work in spite of that. He works through it. When He called us to be His disciple(maker)s, He factored in our ignorance, our personality, our awkwardness, our quirks. God isn't looking for professionals. He's looking for willing participants.

Middles, this is for you. When we talk about unconditional love that changes churches, communities, and nations, it can feel overwhelming. How do we love like that all the time? What happens when we make a mistake? Get mad? Assume? Walk into a social trap? Misunderstand? We can feel so inadequate because we are inadequate. Inevitably, we will mess this up.

That's why we start with understanding God's *agape* love for us. Once we get that, we can rest in His acceptance regardless of our inconsistency. The peace that comes from Him doesn't free us to treat people with indifference. We are instead prompted to love others the same way as often as we can. The

Father loves us, the Spirit guides us, Jesus shows us what it looks like and saves us from ourselves when we fall short.

Every time we get it right, we bring heaven down here. Every time we get it wrong, heaven intervenes.

THE LEAST OF US

In the last week of His life, Jesus was in Jerusalem teaching. His disciples were still unclear about what was to happen. They only knew they were following the Messiah and that He was promising a kingdom. Their minds were perhaps still clouded with the idea of a temporal, earthly kingdom and the places of prominence available in the Messiah's government.

They weren't in tune with heaven yet.

Right after Jesus points out the widow putting her last two coins in the treasury, He takes the boys out of the Temple. One of them, thinking of the majesty of the Messiah's rule, marvels at the beauty of that building (Mark 13:1). Shockingly, Jesus predicts the impending destruction of that Temple. How could this be? The two sets of brothers, Peter and Andrew, James and John, are trying to figure out what it all means (Mark 13:3). By this time, they know all they need to do is ask.

> *As he sat on the Mount of Olives, the disciples came to him privately, saying, "Tell us, when will these things be, and what will be the sign of your coming and of the end of the age?"*
>
> — *Matthew 24:3*

I'm less interested in interpreting the next thirty verses than I am in seeing where Jesus ends up. Though we could have some great conversation about the signs He mentions, I think we miss the point when we dwell on them. Instead, I find it interesting that He spends more time (the next 65 verses) telling us how to live than He does telling us what's going to happen.

> *"From the fig tree learn its lesson: as soon as its branch becomes tender and puts out its leaves, you know that summer is near. So also, when you see all these things, you know that He is near, at the very gates."*
>
> — *Matthew 24:32-33*

> *"But concerning that day and the hour no one knows, not even the angels of heaven, nor the Son, but the Father only.*
>
> — *Matthew 24:36*

> *"Watch therefore, for you know neither the day nor the hour."*
>
> — *Matthew 25:13*

> *"For to everyone who has will more be given, and he will have an abundance. But from the one who has not, even what he has will be taken away."*
>
> — *Matthew 25:29*

Jesus doesn't discount the question of His four followers. He answers with some specifics, even if they are vague to us. This is the only time in Scripture where I picture Jesus the way Hollywood does—looking off into the distance, eyes shining, thoughtful expression, otherworldly. He is staring down the corridors of the future and knows exactly what He is seeing.

Can He share it exactly as He sees it with the brothers? Impossible. They don't have the frame of reference to understand. When He finishes, I imagine Him coming back to them and realizing that if He leaves the conversation unfinished, they will miss the point. Gently, He leads them down a path.

- **Watch for the signs.** We are not to shy away from interpreting the signs Jesus gave us. Just as a good farmer knows how to read the seasons, we are to read the seasons of this spiritual journey.
- **But don't get hung up on them.** Sometimes, we get carried away trying to figure out what the future is. When we do this, we stop being effective in the present. The point of the signs is to tell us that we will readily see when time grows short. The response can't be to find out how much time is left. Instead, it should give us a sense of urgency.
- **Instead, let's stay prepared.** Jesus wants to make sure we are ready ourselves. We aren't to be so focused on others that we forget to keep the peace He has given us. Staying personally prepared isn't selfish. Self-soul-care is vital for our effectiveness as we reach out with the Gospel.

- **Then, we can make the most of every opportunity.** The parable of the talents teaches us so much we could probably do a book together just on those seventeen verses. For the moment, though, let's focus on the surface. God has given us His unconditional love and grace, a great gift that He expects us to invest. The more we invest it, the more He is willing to give us.

The answer the disciples have been waiting to hear really comes at the end of the teaching, but it still isn't what they expect. I believe they were interested in when the Temple would fall, but I think they were truly curious about the Kingdom they were serving. What would it look like? How could it exist if the Temple was gone? What did this mean for them?

How long did they have to suffer to get to the good stuff?

"When the Son of Man comes in His glory, and all the angels with Him, then He will sit on His glorious throne. Before Him will be gathered all the nations, and He will separate people one from another as a shepherd separates the sheep from the goats."

— *Matthew 25:32-33*

Yes! Here it is! The moment they've all been serving to see! The Messiah on His throne, the nations groveling at His feet, the separation of the Jews from the rest of the world! We knew it!

Only they didn't know it. Jesus gave some clues here. The Son of Man, it seems, is going to come again (*When the Son of Man comes in His glory*), and when He does, His army will not be humans (*and all the angels with Him*). He's not separating Jews from the rest (*a shepherd separates the sheep from the goats*). The image Jesus gives them is of His Second Coming after His ascension, but they don't understand that yet.

Still, here's the good stuff. Right? Jesus wins. He sits on His throne. He gathers His people. Now that we see through the lens of history, we know what He means, right? We win! We get to be a part of it! The good life awaits!

Only Jesus wasn't talking about the good life. He was talking about the God life. He was preparing us as disciple (maker)s for what would transpire during our lifetimes. Not the end times. Our times. The same Jesus who described this magnificent triumph also warned us about the life we would live.

"And then many will fall away and betray one another and hate one another. And many false prophets will arise and lead many astray. And because lawlessness will be increased, the love of many will grow cold."
— *Matthew 24:10-12*

Tribulation is coming our way. Hate. False teachers. Falling away. Lawlessness. And because all these things will be true, the worst thing that could happen to the world will happen. The *agape* love of many will grow cold. The Greek word used

243

for growing cold literally means to be blown out, like a candle that shed light and warmth suddenly being snuffed out by a gust of air. Unconditional love will cease.

Imagine a world that lives that way. People will look out mostly for themselves. Even when they love, they will love for what they get and not for what they can give. They will be jealous of what others have and be offended if they can't have it. The rules will be remade to fit their selfish desires. Nothing will be sacred anymore, and no one will be exempt from their contempt. Serving will be for the good it makes them feel and for the service they expect in return. Soon, even the most basic things will be twisted to fit their definition of happiness.

Sounds like the world today, doesn't it?

Sounds like some of our churches today, too…

What is the cure?

"Then the King will say to those on His right, 'Come, you who are blessed by my Father, inherit the Kingdom prepared for you from the foundation of the world. For I was hungry and you gave Me food, I was thirsty and you gave Me drink, I was a stranger and you welcomed Me, I was naked and you clothed Me, I was sick and you visited Me, I was in prison and you came to Me.'"

— *Matthew 25:34-36*

Makes me want to say, "Hold on a minute, my King. Nations have fallen before You. The right to separate the sheep from the goats is Yours. You are the Messiah-King, the Prophet-

Priest, the One we've been expecting. When were you in such a bad spot that you were hungry, thirsty, estranged, naked, sick, or imprisoned? Far be it from me to let You find yourself in such a low place!"

I see bright, moist eyes shining from the soft face of Jesus as He smiles. He knows I'm close to understanding how to love Him, but He also knows I'm still far from understanding to love Him is to love each other. I'm wanting to give Him the best of my earthly love, to fill my chorus with as much *philos* for Him that He accepts me for His.

Peter was there, too. When the leader of the apostles was restored after denying Jesus, he was asked three times by his King if Peter loved him.

"Peter, do you *agape* Me more than these?"

"Yes, my King, I *philos* you."

"Feed my lambs." (John 21:15-17)

Just as He did with Peter, Jesus is calling you and me to a higher love than what we can accomplish on our own. A heavenly love with a heavenly perspective that allows us to be heavenly to those around us. Can we answer that call?

Only if we stop using the phrase *the least of these.* This is subtle, but I believe it is the key to *agape.* In this passage, Jesus is talking as King when He says the following:

> *"And the King will answer them, 'truly, I say to you, as you did it to one of the least of these My brothers, you did it to Me.'"*

> — *Matthew 25:40*

245

But He's the King. When He says *the least of these*, you and I are one of them! I am hungry sometimes for something more. I thirst for understanding. I feel isolated and alone. I feel naked and vulnerable. I am sick of myself sometimes, sick of the world, sick of the church, sick of my shortcomings. I am imprisoned by my sin and my strongholds.

I am the least of us.

Agape doesn't see as we see. This kind of love has an eternal perspective. *Agape* sees us as we are, which allows us to see others as they are. The service we provide them comes from the *agape* God has for us through Jesus and the Spirit He places in us to love the least of us even when it is difficult.

If we are to *agape* God with all our hearts, all our souls, and all our minds, then we must use all our strength—our resources, our bodies, our whole selves—to serve the least of us as if we are one of the least of us, too.

I'm not better than the homeless person. I am just as hungry for righteousness.

I'm not better than the alcoholic. I am just as thirsty for an escape.

I'm not better than the social outcast. I am just as isolated from my best self.

I'm not better than the vulnerable victim. I am just as naked in my guilt.

I'm not better than the physically sick and disabled. I am just as spiritually disabled.

I'm not better than the convict. I am just as guilty.

I hope you are thinking of the Beatitudes in Matthew 5:2-12.

When I see myself for who I am without Jesus, then I can see the least of us as my brother and my sister. But *agape* doesn't stop there. When I start seeing myself for who I am *with* Jesus, I realize I can't keep that to myself.

I realize that I can't be so selfish as to be a disciple. No other choice is left to me. I must be a disciple-maker.

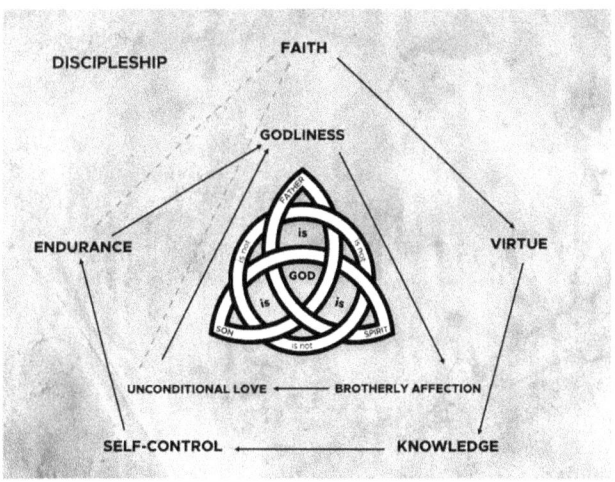

The Next Thing

Maybe you feel a little cheated. I said this book was about making disciples, and it seems like I focused on what it means for *you* to be a disciple. Well, in a way, that's true. To make a disciple, you must first understand what it means to be one. In *Rethink*, we talked about repenting of our frustration with the church and looking for answers. In *Follow*, we talked about what the Gospel is and what it means for us to commit to it. In this volume, we've built on those first two lessons in a very structured way.

To be disciple(maker)s, we must:

1. **Believe God can heal the church.** We have to stop falling for the lie that the Church is doomed and that nothing can be done about it. We need to become expressions of God, but let God do His work and focus on the work He has given us.

2. **Believe disciple-making is attainable for me.** None of us are exempt from this calling. We may not be the go-getter, but that's okay. God uses those of us who are Middles just as much as He does those Type-A's. We need to believe God wants to work through us, too. How? By turning us into expressions of Him (not by turning them into expressions of us!).

3. **The Great Commission is to share the Good News through the Great Commandments.** We can no longer pretend we don't know what the mission is. God has given us His most prized tools to help us and told us to start working right where we are to love people into the Gospel.

4. **His godly dynamite has bestowed upon us all the things we need for all our lives to be devoted to Him.** So we start with believing Him (faith) and let it change us (virtue) until we crave understanding Him intimately (knowledge) and submit to His control (self-control) even if it costs us everything (steadfastness).

5. **So we live in His Presence for God, for the church, and for the world.** Our devotion to God reveals the grace we need to love our brothers and sisters in Christ, which is practice so that we can love the one in front of us.

6. **We see heaven to be heavenly and bring heaven here.** Our new perspective allows us to see ourselves as part of "the least of us" so that we see the kindred

spirits in the church and the craving spirits outside the church as opportunities to love, not judge.

What now? If we repent (rethink) how we interact with God, the church, and the world, then give our allegiance (faith) to Jesus, recognizing His mission is to make us disciple(maker)s, what is next?

Glad you asked.

In the next volume, it's time to talk about what it means to gather with other saints and create communities that invite others to be disciple(maker)s. If you are still frustrated, don't get anxious. I'm not going to pretend the church has no problems. I'm not going to act like gathering will be easy just because I wrote a few books and told everybody what to do. I'm not going to tell you that Sunday morning services are still the answer.

I know this is going to be difficult. Just look at the history of our faith. Honestly? Just look at the Scripture we profess to be inspired by the Holy Spirit. Jealousy, false teaching, favoritism, wrong doctrine, poor leadership . . . the main reason we have the writings we have is partly due to the way the church was acting just years after Jesus died.

We won't fix it this side of heaven. But we can choose to be one of the least of us who sees how heavenly the Church can be.

Maybe, too, we can bring some heaven into her.

For Rethinking Followers Who Choose to Become Discicple (Maker)S:

Now that we've come to an agreement on what it means to be on mission for Christ, it's time for some practical steps. In the first two volumes, I followed up the main text with questions about each section. You'll see a shortened version of that below.

The best way to make the most of what you've read, though, is to watch my television channel, Filled To Empty, on Roku TV and Amazon Fire. Seasons one and two explore my first book, *Rethink*, which is helpful for background and better understanding.

Season three is a video representation of this book. With it, we have added a free workbook to our website, www.filledto-empty.tv, to help you explore disciple-making with others who are also interested in the mission Jesus gave us. Gather a few like-minded individuals to pray for God's direction, watch an episode, talk about what you've learned, and use the workbook throughout the week to enforce that learning.

When you gather, one way to approach your meetings is to learn to STAND FIRM in Christ, as Paul tells us in his letter to the Ephesians:

> *Therefore take up the whole armor of God, that you may be able to withstand in the evil day, and having done all, to STAND FIRM. STAND therefore . . .*
> *— Ephesians 6:13-14a, capitalization mine*

An outline of STAND FIRM follows these questions, but please don't skip this section. The answers to these questions will help prepare you for this new endeavor.

INTRODUCTION

1. Is God calling you to more than what you've experienced before? How would you know?
2. What is the difference between the actions of a disciple and the actions of a disciple-maker?

PART 1: KNOW: TENSION

1. What are the biggest issues about the church that frustrate you and make it difficult for you to trust her? Do you believe God can fix her?

2. Since you *are* the church, what are you doing that might frustrate others in the church and make it difficult for them to trust you? Do you believe God can fix you?

PART 1: KNOW: TEACHING

1. Are you a Type-A or a Middle? (If you *were* an Other before you read this book, my prayer is that you've at least moved to Middle!) As a Type-A, what have you learned about the Middles? As a Middle, what have you learned about yourself?
2. Would you add anything to The Great Commission of spreading the Gospel through The Great Commandments? Any other non-negotiables for you in Scripture?

PART 2: BE: BELIEVE

1. This is where your Testimony lives. How has our extraordinary God moved in your real life?
2. What attributes of God convince us that He can move today? How do we show that we trust Him to make those moves?

PART 2: BE: BECOME

1. What steps can you take to become a Grace Agent in your world?
2. How will becoming a Grace Agent change your character and your reputation?

PART 3: LIVE: HEART

1. What part of your life is still causing you shame? Remember, guilt is "I've done something wrong," and shame is "There's something wrong with me."
2. If God is willing to forgive what you've done, what authority do you have to continue to beat yourself up about it?

SOUL

1. How would your life change if you believed God will, not just that God can?
2. What is God asking you to become? How can you identify with *that* instead of what you are afraid you will become?

MIND

1. Is there any way to really *know* Jesus without spending time with His Body? Not just know about Him. *Know* (epignosis) Him. Could you know me without spending time around my physical presence?
2. Jesus chose the Church (other disciple-makers) as His physical presence today. Can you get to know (epignosis) Him if you don't spend any time in His physical presence?
3. If biblical self-control is really submission, what part do we play in that?
4. What ways can you prepare yourself to endure the hardships that can come from standing firm for your faith?

STRENGTH

1. What part of your life do you need help giving to God? Have you tried doing it on your own? Are you willing to admit you need another brother (the Church) to succeed?
2. Are you still struggling with repenting of (rethinking) your frustration with the Church? How can you take the next step in forgiving and coming alongside your brothers and sisters?

3. To follow, we must submit our own thoughts and feelings about the world and see things from God's heavenly perspective. What steps can you take to adopt that kind of vision?

From Disciple to Disciple-Maker

As a lead pastor, I can't tell you how many new initiatives I've begun in a church. We did Rick Warren's *40 Days of Purpose* and a whole plan based on Craig Groeschel's *It: How Churches and Leaders Can Get It and Keep It*. I've led a church to *Be the Message* (Chris & Kerry Shook) and *Multiply* (David Platt & Francis Chan). Every one of them has had a positive impact on the congregation I led. Every one of them died a slow and sometimes painful death.

Why?

Nothing wrong with any of them. All of them are biblically based; none of them required us to be tied to a denomination. We set a plan that usually included a sermon series, a kickoff event, six to twelve weeks of small group participation, and leadership buy-in. Type-A's jumped on them and Middles shrugged their shoulders and set themselves to the task. The impact was measurable and then miserable.

I'm self-aware enough to realize some of this is my leadership. I've struggled to keep up the original enthusiasm in my congregations. The leadership and the Type-A's want it to succeed, but it requires the quiet, steady support of the Middles to do so. Marketing works on Middles to try out a new thing. Eventually, however, we need sure, steady sustainability to commit long-term.

At the same time, success is what keeps the Type-A's involved. When they see the effort waning, they don't always (usually?) think of how to help with the momentum. Instead, they look for the new thing they can use that might have better success.

Without a sustainable program, engaging the Middles becomes impossible. Without a new program, engaging Type-A's becomes impossible. The former shrug their shoulders at the next new thing and the Type-A's wonder how long *this one* is going to work.

The worst part? All the preaching and marketing that led up to the first steps of those programs. We promise this one is going to work, this one is going to stick, this one is going to be the one that changes the church. And it does, briefly before it doesn't. So we go to the next one and do the same process.

LEADERS ARE OFTEN AS TIRED AS YOU ARE

What we want more than anything is to serve one more, reach one more, teach one more, and help one more grow in Christ. Just as the congregation can be fatigued by the continual search for the next new thing, so leaders can find themselves unable to get excited about yet another chance to revolutionize the church.

Why is this so hard? We all want to see our church mature into what Christ intended His Bride to become. Why can't we sustain it?

Some of this is human nature. We may say we want change, but when we must work to create change or have to submit to accept change, we balk. Sustaining change is even more difficult because the old roads still have the ruts from the wagons we were using before.

Look it up. Our railroad rails are the same width as our wagon wheels. Our wagon wheels were the same width as chariot wheels. Chariot wheels were the exact width of two horses' rumps so that each chariot could be driven across Rome. Our railroad tracks today were determined by two horses' backs in the time of the Roman Empire.

Even when we change, we struggle to really change.

This is why it's so easy to believe in the stronghold that revival today is impossible. So what's the answer? How can we avoid this trap and see real life in the church again?

Well, look around. We may chastise ourselves for never finding the eternal fix, but that's because we are relying on ourselves to produce the eternal fix. Instead, let's see the cycles and processes of the Church as a necessary refreshing to bring more to awareness and life. If I expect to find or create a method that works until Jesus comes back, I am going to be disappointed.

Instead, I must see the constant revision of the church as a necessary work of God as He refuses to give up on us. He sends

His prophets and teachers, His evangelists and shepherds, His apostles—if you will—who provide us new railroads to take us to spiritual maturity.

I say all this so that we avoid the expectation that what I'm about to share will work from now until the Second Coming. However, this is based on what we've learned from Peter, and I believe it has a sound biblical foundation. This method will work with a micro-group, a small group, a Wednesday believer's gathering, or a Sunday morning gathering. It teaches us to stand firm in the faith (allegiance) and be a disciple-maker no matter how we gather.

Find at least two others willing to try it. Each time you get together, follow this format for your meeting:

STAND

Submit to God – James 4:1-10 (dypsychoi – two souls, two identities)
Talk about life – 2 Corinthians 13:
Assess each other – 1 John 3:16-24
Nourish each other's faith – 1 John 4:7-12
Defend each other's holiness – 1 John 5:1-4

As you meet, remember the purpose, the process, the power, and the privilege it is to be the church:

FIRM

- **FORMATIONAL** – The purpose of each meeting is to mature each disciple. Although good relationships and good study help, we must remember those are tools God uses to bring about the maturation we seek. They are not the purpose; maturity is.

- **INTENTIONAL** – The process of maturing disciples is to focus on making disciples. We must do this on purpose because it's easy to go back to those old wagon ruts of focusing on knowledge, relationship, or self-control.

- **RELATIONAL** – the power that allows making disciples to be possible is a relationship, first with God and then with each other. This sounds contradictory to the first two points, but what we've done is put relationship in its proper place. Relationship is built on trust, trust is built on honesty and forgiveness. We must learn how to be honest with God, with ourselves, and with each other. The best way to do that is with people we trust.

- **MISSIONAL** – making disciples of each other and reaching out to include more disciples is a privilege as much as a duty. Remember that when it gets difficult or feels impossible. We don't *have* to do this; we *get* to do this. Disciple-making requires reaching and training others, but let's remember it's a joy, not a chore.

In the next volume, we'll revisit these ideas and learn what it means to gather the church together to become disciple-makers. In doing so, I believe we will rediscover what it means to be the "called out ones." The *ekklesia*. The Church.

Appendix A

AN EXERCISE TO RELEASE SHAME

To make it easier for you to do this exercise, I have included the instructions here:

1. Go through both lists and circle the personal and corporate sins you have committed.
2. Go back through and put a star on the circled ones that you can't help repeating.
3. Go back through and put a box around the ones with stars that make you experience shame: feeling wearied, tormented, darkened, defiled, and weakened.
4. Rip out the pages, turn them sideways, and rip them in half.
5. Try to put the pages back together. Notice that nothing, not even glue or tape, will make them whole again. That's what sin is doing to you in your life.

6. Open the Bible to Psalm 51 and either place it before you or prepare yourself to read it for your group. If you are leading a group, don't hold the Bible in your hands—do the exercise with your group members.

7. Take pages in each hand, crumple them, and hold them as tightly as you can. That's how we hold onto the shame we feel from our sin.

8. READ PSALM 51 OUT LOUD for yourself (and the group. You might have everyone read it together out loud, but it's a long passage). Don't read it silently. Scripture was written to be read out loud.

9. When you sense God's grace over your sin, release the pages from your fists. Feel the release of tension in your hands. That's how your soul feels when you stop beating yourself up for the things you've done.

10. When we first taught this, we had everyone put all the sins into a container and set them on fire to show they were no longer our concern. Be careful with this if you are inside!

11. Take some time and reflect quietly on what just happened. Then pray and praise God for your deliverance from shame.

PERSONAL SINS

Sexual immorality – porneia – (4) selling your sexual purity

Impurity – akathartos – (3) foul, unclean, impure emotional state

    Catharsis cleans out your emotions. A-catharsis keeps them dirty.

Passion – pathos – depraved longing

    This is the root of "Pathological" (compulsive, obsessive)

Evil desire – kaken epithymian – Eagerness for evil things

Idolaters – eidolotrai – worship of images, icons, not-gods

Adulterers – moichoi – one who has sex outside marriage

Effeminate – malakos – soft, womanly

    A metaphor used in that day for displaying the body lewdly.

Greedy – pleonektai

Drunkards – methysoi – exactly what the English says

Sensuality – aselgia – conduct shocking to public decency more than dressing lewdly. Acting lewdly in public.

Sorcery – pharmakeia – magic, enchantment
Where we get "pharmacy" and Include the use of drugs

Jealousy – zelos – emotion bubbling over
Greeks thought water bubbling over sounded like this.

Envy – phthonoi – really better translated as grudges, or spite.

Filthiness – aischrotes – obscenity, indecency, baseness

Crude joking – eutrapelia – just what it says

Lovers of self – philautoi – selfishness

Lovers of money – philargyroi – money-loving, monetary greed

Proud – hyperephanoi – disdainful of other people
Treating people like we are superior

Arrogant – alazones – boastful, loud, flaunting

Disobedient – apeithes – unbelieving and so disobedient

Ungrateful – acharistoi – can't be pleased, won't thank others

Unholy – anosioi – regarding nothing as sacred

Without self-control – akrateis – inclined to excess, gluttony

Reckless – propeteis – impulsive, rash, headstrong

Swollen with conceit – tetyphomenoi – properly to blow smoke

Lovers of pleasure – philedonoi – what it says, "hedonism."

Appearing godly but denying its power – morphosin eusebeias –
Pretending to worship God but denying His power.

CORPORATE SINS

Covetousness – pleonexian – (2) Avarice, aggression

Having a desire for advantage over people.

Anger – orgen – anger that desires vengeance

Wrath – thymon – outbursts from rage

Malice – kakian – wishing evil on people, spiteful, vicious.

Slander – blasphemian – abusive or scurrilous language.

Lying about people to hurt them. Reversing moral realities.

Obscene talk – aischrologian – filthy speech, foul language

Lying – pseudesthe – to speak falsely, tell an untruth to deceive.

Thieves – kleptai – one who steals by stealth rather than violence

We get "kleptomaniac" from this word.

Revilers – loidoroi – One who rails at people, abuses them.

Swindlers – harpages – extortion, robbery, stealing by violence.

Enmity – echthrai – hostility, alienating people (bullying)
Purposely acting in an abusive way to make another isolated.

Strife – eris – contention, creating quarrels
Loving to cause disputes and fights.

Rivalries – eritheiai – seeking followers
Creating cliques and using them to create feuds or faction

Dissensions – dichostasiai – standing apart
Choosing wrongly not to stand with the group.

Divisions – haireseis – self-chosen opinion that creates discord

Orgies – komoi – partying with unbridled sexual immorality

Foolish talk – morologia – dull, without edge talk "moron," losing edge on reality, talking without meaning
The result of a sluggish mind, not thinking about what you say

Abusive to parents – blasphemoi goneusin

Heartless – astorgoi – unloving, no love for mankind

Unappeasable – aspondoi – unforgiving despite apology

Slanderous – diaboloi – falsely accusing

Brutal – anemeroi – savage in how you treat others

Not loving good – aphilagathoi – hostile to the things of God
Not accepting the good of someone

Treacherous – prodotai – traitor, one who betrays a trust.

Slanders – katalaliai – evil speaking, backbiting

Gossip – psithurismoi – whispering, secret attacks on character.

Other Books
By Michael S. Rogers

PASSING LINCOLN. Modern day telling of what happens to the widow's two mites after she puts them in the treasury (Mark 12:42-44). Tag line: Small gifts go a long way.

WILL CHANGERS (series). Spiritual thrillers of the end times.

DARK FORCES RISING (book 1). Four people gifted with the ability to see the Will of God and battle demons to bring it about are confronted by a new enemy.

UNHOLY TRINITY (book 2). The Will Changers find out their real enemy—three evil Will Changers with a penchant for destruction.

WISDOM BEYOND HIS YEARS (e-book only). Lessons I learned from my firstborn son.